IMAGES
of Rail

AKRON RAILROADS

Akron Union Depot opened in 1950, culminating decades of efforts by Akron civic leaders to prod the railroads into creating a new station to replace an outdated facility built in 1891. However, passenger trains were entering a twilight era and by the time this photograph of the westbound Baltimore and Ohio *Diplomat* was taken on January 3, 1970, only four passenger trains used the station. (Photograph by John Beach.)

On the cover: A trio of Q class 2-8-2 Mikados pause at Valley Yard on the former Cleveland Terminal and Valley Railroad line in 1955. The Mikados had distinctive Vanderbilt tenders. Valley Yard, located north of Akron Junction, had four tracks and room for 120 cars. The Valley line's other yard, Hazel Street Yard, had nine tracks and a 140-car capacity. (Photograph by Bob Redmond.)

IMAGES
of Rail

AKRON RAILROADS

Craig Sanders

ARCADIA
PUBLISHING

Published by Arcadia Publishing
Charleston, South Carolina

Library of Congress Catalog Card Number: 2006935206

For all general information contact Arcadia Publishing at:
Telephone 843-853-2070
Fax 843-853-0044
E-mail sales@arcadiapublishing.com
For customer service and orders:
Toll-Free 1-888-313-2665

Visit us on the Internet at www.arcadiapublishing.com

Robert W. Richardson (right) and three other men formed a committee in 1936 that would evolve into the Akron Railroad Club. Richardson is the last surviving cofounder. J. Gary Dillon (left) joined the club in June 1947 and has been an officer longer than any other club member. Currently the vice president, Dillon also served as treasurer and president. (Courtesy of Akron Railroad collection.)

CONTENTS

ACKNOWLEDGMENTS

Celebrating its 70th anniversary in 2006, the Akron Railroad Club is an organization of railroad enthusiasts sharing their mutual passion for railroad operations and history at monthly meetings, on field trips, and through friendship. Akron Railroad Club members have dutifully chronicled Ohio's changing railroad scene, watching as steam locomotives gave way to diesels, interurban railways vanished, and intercity rail passenger service withered to almost nothing. They have seen the railroad industry undergo a massive transformation and witnessed a revival unforeseen in the 1970s, when many eastern railroads were bankrupt or on the verge of financial failure.

This book provides a look at those changes with a nod toward the early history of the railroads of Akron and Summit County. I created this book to help celebrate 70 years of the Akron Railroad Club and to document Akron's colorful railroad heritage.

I would like to thank the following club members who provided photographs for this book: Richard Antibus, John Beach, Peter Bowler, Alex Bruchac, Dennis Bydash, John B. Corns, J. Gary Dillon, Roger Durfee, Ben Eubank, Bob Farkas, Richard Jacobs, Robert MacCallum, Bob Redmond, Edward Ribinskas, Robert Rohal, John Schon, H. Vaughn Smith, Marty Surdyk, and John Wunderle. Carl Ehmann searched out photographs for me from the University of Akron archives and the Cuyahoga Falls Public Library. Other club members who provided information or assistance include Robert Richardson, Dennis Tharp, and Jim Weyrich.

Also providing photographs or assistance were James Spangler, Dan Davidson, William Kuethe Jr., and Sheldon Lustig. Chuck Blardone of the Pennsylvania Railroad Technical and Historical Society arranged for the use of photographs from that society's archives. Paul Vernier allowed me to photograph artifacts from his collection.

I would also like to thank Melissa Basilone, my editor at Arcadia Publishing, and publisher John Pearson for their assistance by answering my many questions. Finally this book would not have been possible without the assistance of my wife, Mary Ann Whitley, who copyedited the manuscript and provided encouragement and support throughout. The responsibility for any errors or omissions lies solely with the author.

INTRODUCTION

Canals were instrumental in Akron's creation, but railroads were key to its development, both as an industrial center and as the world's rubber capital. Founded in 1825 by Gen. Simon Perkins and Paul Williams, Akron was located on the Ohio and Erie and the Pennsylvania and Ohio Canals. Akron derived its name from a Greek word meaning high, while Summit County reflected the area's location at the crest of the Ohio and Erie Canal.

Even before completion of the canals, some argued that Akron needed a railroad in order to thrive. A committee formed in 1832 sought financing for a survey for the Great Western Railway between the Hudson River and the Portage Summit, but the road never developed. Plans for the Akron and Perrysburg, Akron and Richmond, and Akron and Canton Railroads likewise were stillborn.

Summit County's first railroad, the Cleveland and Pitssburg Railroad Company (C&P), missed Akron by 15 miles. Chartered in 1836, financial problems delayed construction until the early 1850s. The C&P opened between Cleveland and Wellsville on March 4, 1852, operating through Macedonia, Hudson, Alliance, and Bayard.

The railroad triggered an economic boom in Hudson, Summit County's oldest city, and some Akronites feared falling behind. Col. Simon Perkins Jr., a state senator and son of Akron's cofounder, led a delegation to Columbus to prod the Ohio legislature into amending the C&P charter. The legislature obliged on February 19, 1851, directing the C&P to construct a branch from Hudson via Akron, to a connection with the Ohio and Pennsylvania Railroad between Wooster and Massillon.

With the railroad's cost estimated at $1 million, Colonel Perkins and others also persuaded the legislature to require Summit County to buy $100,000 of stock, subject to voter approval. Opponents decried public funding of a railroad, saying canals and stagecoaches adequately met Akron's transportation needs. The issue passed 2,432 to 1,605 in a referendum held June 21, 1851. Eight townships voted against it, but the vote was 737-3 in favor in Akron and 275-12 in favor in Cuyahoga Falls.

The railroad reached Cuyahoga Falls on June 1, 1852. The route into Akron followed the Pennsylvania and Ohio Canal to about a quarter mile west of Old Forge, where it began a southerly trajectory toward Summit Street, while skirting Akron's southern boundary. Just as geography had influenced canal operations, Akron's two major east–west railroads, the Baltimore and Ohio (B&O) and the Erie, later would cut through the heart of Akron on a generally north–south orientation.

Construction crews worked overtime to reach Akron by Sunday, July 4, 1852. Swarms of volunteers aided the tired workers on Saturday. Despite laws prohibiting labor on Sunday, the last spike was driven an hour after midnight. City leaders had planned to celebrate completion of the railroad on Monday, but the first locomotive to chug into Akron arrived in the wee hours of Sunday morning with its whistle blowing. A church bell tolled, and cannons boomed. Hundreds of people spilled into the streets, ignoring the lateness of the hour and laws against such behavior on the Sabbath. Karl Grismer, author of Akron and Summit County, wrote that "old timers related that nearly all of the grog shops in town opened wide their doors, just to help the merrymakers become a little merrier."

The celebration hardly slowed on Monday. "The town was crowded from morning till evening by visitors from all sections of the county, anxious to receive their first introduction to a locomotive," the Akron Beacon reported. More than 2,000 rode a special train of two passenger coaches and several flat cars that made five Akron–Hudson round-trips. A cannon mounted on a flat car fired repeatedly. Pulling the train was the wood-burning locomotive Vulcan, which traveled at the amazing speed of 25 miles per hour. Conductor Isaac Lewis was a former canal boat captain.

Building of the Akron branch continued southward, with a connection to the Ohio and Pittsburgh being made at Orrville. Construction halted at Millersburg. The Akron branch was renamed Cleveland, Zanesville and Cincinnati (CZ&C) on March 17, 1853. Following an 1861 foreclosure, the receiver sold the CZ&C to George W. Cass and John J. Marvin, who in turn conveyed it to the Pittsburg, Fort Wayne and Chicago Railway (successor to the Ohio and Pittsburgh), which the Pennsylvania Railroad leased in perpetuity on June 27, 1869. However, the Pennsylvania Railroad sold the CZ&C to the Pittsburgh, Mount Vernon, Columbus and London Railroad, which completed the route between Millersburg and Columbus on September 1, 1873, and operated it as the Cleveland, Mount Vernon and Delaware Railroad.

The Cleveland, Mount Vernon and Delaware defaulted in 1881, and ownership bounced through the courts until the company emerged December 31, 1885, as the Cleveland, Akron and Columbus Railway Company. The original destination of the Akron branch had been Zanesville, which finally was reached May 27, 1888. The Zanesville route, known as the Dresden branch, diverged at Killibuck. The Pennsylvania Railroad gained control of the Cleveland, Akron and Columbus Railway's capital stock in 1899.

The jubilation of gaining a railroad in 1852 had scarcely diminished before Akron leaders were working to attract a second railroad. Akron had not been the only town irked at being bypassed by the C&P. In nearby Franklin Mills, businessman Marvin Kent was so upset over the C&P passing two miles to the north that, legend has it, he worked full time at bringing a New York–St. Louis broad-gauge railroad to town, the Atlantic and Great Western Railroad (A&GW). The A&GW was the brainchild of eastern investors in the Erie Railroad and their British financiers. Their goal was to build between the Erie at Salamanca, New York, and the Cincinnati, Hamilton and Dayton Railroad at Dayton.

Railroad building in the mid-19th century required procuring charters from state legislatures, many of which were suspicious of railroad barons who in turn did not want to tip off their competitors about their plans. The investors recruited local businessmen, such as Kent and his father, Zenas Kent, to front for them in dealing with the legislature. A&GW backers also enlisted the support of Akronites Colonel Perkins, Lucius V. Bierce, Harvey B. Spelman, and Dr. Daniel Upson. They told the Ohio legislature that the proposed Coal Hill Railroad planned to haul coal between Tallmadge and the C&P in Trumbull County.

In 1854, after charters had been secured in Ohio, Pennsylvania, and New York, the A&GW revealed its true intentions. Marvin Kent served as president of the A&GW of Ohio, of which he was a major stockholder, and turned the first shovel of earth at Franklin Mills on July 4, 1853, to begin building the Ohio Division. A lack of financing that was triggered by a national depression, however, soon halted construction.

After European financiers pledged funding, construction resumed in 1862. The A&GW opened to Ravenna on December 10, 1862, and Akron on May 26, 1863. Kent drove the last spike at Dayton on June 21, 1864, but trains did not operate over the length of the A&GW

until September. Marvin Kent donated 13 acres to establish shops in Franklin Mills, which also became a division headquarters and was renamed Kent on May 6, 1867.

Financier Jay Gould gained control of the Erie Railroad in the late 1860s and, after several failed attempts to acquire a railroad serving Chicago, he leased the A&GW on June 24, 1874. After the A&GW failed to gain control of the Cleveland, Columbus, Cincinnati and Indianapolis Railway (Big Four), the Erie Railroad created a subsidiary company, Chicago and Atlantic, to build between Chicago and Marion, Ohio. Chicago to New York passenger service via Akron began June 17, 1883.

The earliest B&O forerunner in Summit County was the Lake Shore and Tuscarawas Valley Railroad (LS&T). Organized July 2, 1870, the LS&T was completed in August 1873 and had Cleveland and Lorain routes that converged at Lester. The route then continued to Uhrichsville.

The B&O's earliest Akron ancestor was the Valley Railway Company, organized August 21, 1871, to build between Cleveland and the southeastern Ohio coalfields. Construction began in 1873, was suspended during a financial panic a year later, and resumed in 1878. Operations between Cleveland and Canton began February 1, 1880, and to the southern terminus at Valley Junction on January 1, 1883.

The Valley Railway had intended to build to Wheeling, West Virginia, but the Wheeling and Lake Erie Railroad, which reached Valley Junction in August 1892, completed its own line to Martins Ferry (opposite Wheeling) in November 1889. The Valley Railway instead negotiated an agreement with the Wheeling and Lake Erie Railroad in 1896 that enabled each railroad to use the other's tracks between Cleveland and Wheeling.

Following the Civil War, B&O president John W. Garrett concluded that the B&O needed to reach Chicago if it wanted to compete with the Pennsylvania, New York Central, and Erie Railroads for western traffic. A subsidiary company, Baltimore, Pittsburgh and Chicago Railroad, began building between Chicago and Chicago Junction, Ohio (renamed Willard in 1917), in 1873. The route opened November 24, 1874. The Chicago line connected at Chicago Junction with the Sandusky, Mansfield and Newark Railroad, which the B&O had leased. That road connected at Newark with the Central Ohio Railroad, in which B&O held a controlling interest. This created a 784-mile Chicago–Washington route via Wheeling.

The B&O coveted a connecting link between Chicago Junction and Pittsburgh via the industry-rich cities of Akron and Youngstown. It acquired the Pittsburgh and Western Railroad between Pittsburgh and Akron. The Pittsburgh and Western Railroad had begun in the 1870s as a Pennsylvania narrow-gauge line, but had converted to standard gauge by the time it opened to New Castle, Pennsylvania, on January 1, 1883, and reached Akron in 1884.

The Akron and Chicago Junction Railroad was incorporated February 1, 1890, to build between Chicago Junction and Akron. Built eastward, the line reached Clinton on July 1, 1891. The Pittsburgh and Western Railroad had acquired an unused right-of-way between Akron and Clinton that paralleled the Pennsylvania Railroad's Akron–Columbus route. The first train to Pittsburgh departed from Chicago Junction on August 18, 1891, with 18 freighters.

The B&O affiliated with the Valley Railway in January 1890, in order to gain access to Cleveland industrial traffic. The Valley Railway was reorganized October 3, 1895, as the Cleveland Terminal and Valley Railroad Company. After the Wheeling and Lake Erie Railroad acquired the Cleveland, Canton and Southern Railroad in 1899, it cancelled the Cleveland Terminal and Valley Railroad's right to use Wheeling and Lake Erie Railroad tracks between Valley Junction and Wheeling. The Cleveland Terminal and Valley Railroad began using seven miles of the Pennsylvania Railroad between Valley Junction and Dover to reach the former LS&T, now operating as the Cleveland, Lorain and Wheeling Railroad, which had been extended from Uhrichsville to Wheeling in 1880.

Completion of the Chicago Junction–Pittsburgh route gave B&O two paths between Chicago and the East. At the beginning of the 20th century, B&O had two passenger trains between Chicago and New York, one via Akron, and one via Wheeling. By January 1918, however, all Chicago–New York passenger trains operated via Akron, which was about 100 miles shorter.

This also became the preferred route for freight, and the Akron route was double-tracked in the early 20th century.

Four additional railroads were built in the Akron area in the late 19th century. The Pittsburg, Akron and Western Railroad began building eastward from Carey in May 1890, reaching Silver Street in Akron on January 24, 1891. The first passenger train arrived on February 15 of that year. Renamed the Northern Ohio Railway on August 14, 1895, New York Central subsidiary Lake Erie and Western Railroad leased the Northern Ohio Railway on October 1, 1895. The Akron, Canton and Youngstown Railway formed June 6, 1907, and opened between Akron and Mogadore on October 1, 1912. The Akron, Canton and Youngstown Railway leased the Northern Ohio Railway on March 1, 1920.

The Barberton Belt line opened July 12, 1892, between Barberton and a Pennsylvania Railroad connection at South Akron. A route between Cleveland and Creston by the Cleveland, Barberton and Western Railroad (incorporated October 23, 1899) was only constructed between Barberton and a connection with the Northern Ohio Railway at Fairlawn. The Barberton, Akron and Eastern line was incorporated January 24, 1902, to build between Barberton and Youngstown, but fell far short of its goal. These three railroads merged May 6, 1902, to become the Akron and Barberton Belt Railroad. The Akron and Barberton Belt Railroad was extended to East Akron in 1904.

The narrow-gauge Connotton Valley Railway passed just east of Akron through Mogadore, which it reached in January 1881. The line was completed to Cleveland later that year and extended to Zanesville in 1889. The road was converted to standard gauge on November 18, 1888, and renamed the Cleveland, Canton and Southern Railroad on May 17, 1890. The Cleveland, Canton and Southern Railroad entered receivership September 15, 1893, and the Wheeling and Lake Erie Railroad acquired it on August 5, 1899.

With railroads entering Akron from every direction, flour mills, farm implement manufactures, foundries, and rolling mills came to the city to be near the rail lines. This spurred the development of machine tool factories and parts suppliers. Dr. Benjamin Franklin Goodrich moved his rubber factory to Akron in 1871 from Melrose, New York. As the automobile age dawned in the early 20th century, Harvey Firestone convinced Henry Ford to use tires made in Akron. B. F. Goodrich, Firestone, General Tire, and Goodyear Tire and Rubber were soon cranking out thousands of tires for motor vehicles. Akron took off, growing from 69,000 in 1910 to 208,435 in 1920. Railroads brought the raw materials needed to manufacture tires and other durable goods and shipped the finished products all over the country.

Akron's railroad infrastructure remained intact through the early 1970s. The decline of the city's industrial base, coupled with railroad mergers and route rationalizing, prompted the abandonment of some Summit County trackage. Most tire manufacturing in Akron had ended by the 1990s. The county's remaining industries made far less use of rail for shipping. Whereas Akron once had six freight railroads, now there are two. Most of the Erie and Pennsylvania Railroads and parts of the Akron and Barberton Belt Railroad in Akron have been abandoned.

Scheduled intercity rail passenger service in Akron ended May 1, 1971, resumed under Amtrak on November 11, 1990, and ended again on September 10, 1995. It was revived on August 10, 1998 and then discontinued again on March 7, 2005. The Cuyahoga Valley Scenic Railroad operates excursion trains from Akron northward through the Cuyahoga Valley National Park, on track owned by the National Park Service, and between Akron and Canton, on track owned by public agencies in Summit and Stark Counties. Efforts to institute Cleveland-Akron-Canton commuter train service have made little headway.

One

EARLY DAYS AND RAILROAD FACILITIES

Akron's first railroad station was built on Mill Street, near the intersection with Summit Street. Many considered the barn-like structure an eyesore, and two stations replaced it in 1891. The Erie Railroad built a depot just south of the first station while predecessor companies of the Pennsylvania and Baltimore and Ohio (B&O) Railroads opened the second Akron Union Depot on November 1, 1891, between East Market Street and Park Street. Erie Railroad moved to this station on April 23, 1901.

Akron Union Depot was small and soon obsolete. Passenger trains sitting at the station often delayed freight trains. Plans for a third Akron Union Depot were announced in the late 1920s, but the Great Depression and World War II delayed construction until after the war. Erie Railroad built its own station, which opened July 16, 1947, near Exchange and Broadway Streets. The third Akron Union Depot, off Grant Street between Center and Carroll Streets, opened April 28, 1950. A walkway over the tracks connected it with a new Greyhound station on Broadway Street.

The first Valley Railway station was at Howard and Ridge Streets. It was supplemented in 1888 with a larger but short-lived station at Canal and West Market Streets. Trains continued to use the Howard Street station through the final years of passenger service. Akron, Canton and Youngstown (AC&Y) passenger trains used a station on Main Street.

Akron never had large freight classification yards. The B&O yards were located near Akron Junction on the city's east side. The Pennsylvania Railroad's yard was in South Akron while Erie Railroad's McCoy Yard was just southwest of downtown. The AC&Y's Brittain Yard was in East Akron.

The B&O maintained a dispatching office at 39 South Main Street in the Metropolitan Building. Dispatchers controlled the Chicago line between New Castle, Pennsylvania, and Willard, Ohio. This office closed in March 1989 when CSX Transportation opened a central dispatching office in Jacksonville.

Operators at JO Tower on East Market Street controlled the intersection of the Erie Railroad track with the B&O and Pennsylvania Railroad joint line. JO Tower also controlled switches and signals at Akron Union Depot and, after 1967, Akron Junction. JO Tower closed in 1980, and its control functions shifted to Warwick Tower in Clinton.

Many people viewed steam locomotives with a mixture of fear, wonder, and awe. Locomotive engineers and their fellow workers took pride in what they did and posed proudly in front of their locomotives. Valley Railway steam locomotive No. 23 was built in June 1889 by Brooks. The D-18 class 0-6-0T served the B&O until being dropped from the roster in 1920. (Courtesy of Archival Services, University of Akron.)

Built in March 1899 for the B&O Southwestern as No. 286, this H-2 class 2-8-0 was renumbered in 1900. No. 1586 served the B&O for 45 years and had the longest tenure of the 42 locomotives in its class, before being scrapped in April 1944. It is shown at Akron Junction in 1935. (Courtesy of Marty Surdyk collection.)

Brewster Brothers Coal Company operated several mines in the Akron area and used small 0-4-0 steam locomotives to haul minerals from the mines. The crew of the Summit Bank poses in this undated photograph. This locomotive is named for the mine that it and the crew served. (Courtesy of Archival Services, University of Akron.)

Freight cars await loading or unloading in this view of railroading in early-20th-century Akron. The tracks to the right carry trains of the Erie, B&O, and Pennsylvania Railroads. The Erie shops are to the left. Note the majestic twin spires of St. Bernard's Church (far left), built in 1906 with assistance from the king of Prussia. (Courtesy of Archival Services, University of Akron.)

Accidents were common in the 19th century because of shoddy construction and poor safety practices. Operating a steam locomotive could be dangerous, and engineers had to make split-second decisions that made the difference between a close call and catastrophe. Sometimes there was nothing an engineer could do to save his train. The date and place of this derailment on the Northern Ohio Railway are unknown. (Courtesy of Archival Services, University of Akron.)

The most impressive railroad bridge in Akron was the 13-span trestle built in 1891 by the Pittsburg, Akron and Western Railroad over the Ohio Canal. Bridge No. 6, as the railroad knew it, was unusual in that it was of steel construction whereas most Pittsburg, Akron and Western Railroad bridges were built with wood. This trestle was replaced in 1926. (Courtesy of Archival Services, University of Akron.)

Train No. 2 has just arrived in Akron from Delphos, and passengers are embarking at the station on Main Street. Heading the train is Lake Erie and Western No. 5211, a 2-6-0 Mogul assigned to serve the former Northern Ohio Railway route. Although the Lake Erie and Western Railroad leased the Northern Ohio Railway for 999 years, the lease was acquired by the AC&Y in 1920. (Courtesy of Archival Services, University of Akron.)

The second Akron Union Depot was a modest structure that became obsolete after the city entered the rubber era in the second decade of the 20th century. Although five tracks passed the station, waiting passenger trains often held up freight trains. After the opening of the modern Union Depot in 1950, the 1891 station was razed in the summer of 1951. However, in this early-20th-century view, the station was still grand. (Courtesy of Bob Redmond collection.)

The first Valley Railway passenger station in Akron was located at North Howard and Ridge Streets (seen in the photograph above), a location that many Akron residents considered inconvenient. So in 1888, the Valley Railway opened a second Akron station (seen in the photograph below). From a passenger train operations standpoint, this station, located at the southwest corner of West Market and Canal Streets, was a stub end operation and required a backup move into the station for southbound trains or out for northbound trains. Trains rejoined the mainline at Howard Street. Although Valley line passenger trains served both stations, the B&O eventually consolidated Valley line passenger operations at the Howard Street depot. Neither station has survived. (Courtesy of Archival Services, University of Akron.)

The Erie Railroad built this ornate passenger station for $20,000 in 1891. Historian Samuel Lane called the Erie Railroad station "as much of an ornament as the old wooden depot was an eyesore and reproach." Apparently the station's pleasing architecture was not enough for the Erie Railroad, which began using the Akron Union Depot on April 23, 1901. (Courtesy of Archival Services, University of Akron.)

Railroads often spent lavish amounts of money to design and build stations in larger cities, but in many small towns the station was a small, utilitarian structure built to a standard plan. This Erie Railroad station east of Akron in nearby Tallmadge was typical of the many wooden-frame depots of the early 20th century. This view was taken in 1908. (Courtesy of Bob Redmond collection.)

The Pittsburg, Akron and Western Railroad, forerunner of the Northern Ohio Railway, built a yard and engine service facility with a turntable and two-stall engine house near Valley and Silver Streets on Akron's west side. Fire destroyed the engine house on June 19, 1944. In the 1920s, two oil companies and a warehouse were located near the yard. The Silver Street station (seen in the photograph at left) is thought to have been built in the 1920s and was used as a block office for delivery of train orders but never as a passenger station. In the photograph below, AC&Y operator Harry DeForest Keefer stands ready with a P hoop, which was used to hand up train orders to the engine crew. A crew member would grab the hoop, remove the train orders, and toss the hoop onto the ground. (Courtesy of Archival Services, University of Akron.)

Akron's hilly terrain meant that railroads were built through cuts or atop fills. Hence, there were numerous bridges. The Erie, B&O, Pennsylvania, and AC&Y Railroads crossed Forge Street on a cluster of parallel bridges. In the photograph above, looking west in the late 1940s, a B&O steam switcher pauses on the bridge over Forge Street on the middle bridge. The bridge closest to the camera is the AC&Y, which passes beneath the B&O, Pennsylvania, and Erie Railroads to the left out of view. The smokestack belongs to the Renner Brewing Company. The photograph below, taken three decades later, looks eastward. Trains no longer use the Erie Railroad bridge, and that railroad is long gone, but its name and herald still grace this bridge today. (Above, photograph by Bob Redmond; below, photograph by John Beach.)

The Akron Junction track structure resembled a maze. In this late-1940s view looking northward, the track at the far left is the B&O's Valley line between Cleveland and Canton. The track from the lower left corner led to a coaling tower and yard, while the track from the upper left corner connected the Valley line with the Chicago line. (Photograph by Bob Redmond.)

The B&O had one office that served its various freight yards near Akron Junction. The two-story building was located next to the bridge where the Valley line passed beneath the Chicago line, just east of Arlington Street. Although much of the B&O yards are no longer used, the yard office still serves CSX Transportation today. (Photograph by Craig Sanders.)

The Northern Ohio Traction and Light Company opened Akron Terminal Station on June 11, 1918, at Main and Federal (later Perkins) streets. Primarily an interurban railway facility, Akron Terminal Station replaced a storefront station at Main and Mill Streets rendered obsolete by the trend toward multiple-car trains. Akron Terminal Station (seen in the photograph above) was a four-story, white granite building. Aside from a waiting room (seen in the photograph below) and ticket office, Akron Terminal Station featured a newsstand, restaurant, appliance store, baggage locker room, and parking service. Redcaps and doormen were always on duty. The coin-operated lockers and public address system were among the nation's first in a railway station. From here, trains served Cleveland, Ravenna, Canton, and Wadsworth. Located on the northern edge of the Akron business district, Akron Terminal Station rivaled similar facilities in Indianapolis and Milwaukee. (Courtesy of Archival Services, University of Akron.)

Akron's third Union Depot cost $2 million and was dedicated April 28, 1950. Akron officials began pushing for a new station in the 1920s and formed the New Union Depot Civic League to prod the railroads into building it. Their efforts and increased traffic during World War II prompted the Ohio Public Service Commission in 1942 to order a new depot built. The station featured concealed ceiling lights, glass-block windows, and eight divans in the waiting room. Union News Company had a newsstand, and the ticket window was finished with black marble. The concourse over the tracks connected with the Greyhound bus station. The University of Akron later acquired the station complex, which retains much of its original form (seen in the photograph below), although some minor changes and additions have been made. (Photographs by John Beach.)

The Erie Railroad built its own station rather than use the new Akron Union Depot, saying it would be less costly. The 30-by-80-foot masonry structure cost $350,000. Ticketing, the waiting room, and the main entrance were at street level (seen in the photograph above). The photograph below shows the concourse extending from the waiting room over the tracks, as a B&O passenger train passes in June 1965. Passengers used stairways to reach the platforms. The station was dedicated July 16, 1947. Erie Railroad president Robert E. Woodruff presided at a ribbon-cutting ceremony as a Goodyear blimp hovered overhead. The railroad hosted a lunch for 400 community leaders. "No longer will Akronites have to apologize to visitors who come to town on Erie trains," commented the *Akron Beacon Journal*. (Above, photograph by Robert MacCallum; below, photograph by Ben Eubank.)

Ferdinand Schumacher founded the Quaker Oats milling complex in the southeast section of downtown Akron to manufacture rolled oats. Production ended in 1970 when the company moved to Chicago. The building was transformed into Quaker Square, a complex of shops and restaurants, with hotel rooms built into the silos. Situated next to railroad tracks in downtown Akron, some Quaker Square establishments feature a railroad theme. (Photograph by Marty Surdyk.)

JO Tower controlled the crossing of the B&O and Pennsylvania Railroad joint line with the Erie Railroad tracks in downtown Akron. The three-floor tower was built in 1908, into a line of storefronts at East Market and College Streets. The entrance was at street level. Employees of the Pennsylvania Railroad, JO Tower operators controlled movements at Akron Union Depot and the AY interlocking at Akron Junction. The tower closed in 1980. (Photograph by John Beach.)

The B&O and Pennsylvania Railroad joint line and Erie Railroad track crossing at JO Tower was located beneath Mill Street (seen in the photograph above). The sharp angle required moveable point frogs rather than a traditional diamond. The sharpness of the crossing is evident in the photograph below, taken behind a westbound B&O freight train on July 31, 1977, from the East Market Street bridge. Erie Lackawanna Railway owns the two tracks on the left, while B&O and Pennsylvania Railroads jointly used the next two tracks. Pennsylvania Railroad operating rules and timetables governed the joint track, but signals were B&O-style color position lights. Warwick Tower in Clinton controlled the crossing after JO Tower closed. The JO interlocking was removed in 1982 and the tower was razed in the early 21st century during a bridge replacement project. (Above, photograph by John Schon; below, photograph by John Beach.)

The B&O and Pennsylvania Railroad joint line began at Akron Junction and ended at Warwick Tower in Clinton. In the photograph above, the view to the right is toward the B&O yard. The photograph below shows the manipulation chart used by tower operators to line routes by throwing switches and setting signals. The lines in the upper left-hand corner are the joint Pennsylvania Railroad and B&O tracks from Massillon. The line curving to the left is the Pennsylvania Railroad line while the lines curving to the right are B&O. The lines at the upper right side represent the Pennsylvania Railroad route from Columbus, while the lines in the lower right-hand corner are the B&O yard and route from Chicago. The lines in the lower left corner make up the joint line from Akron. (Photographs by Richard Jacobs.)

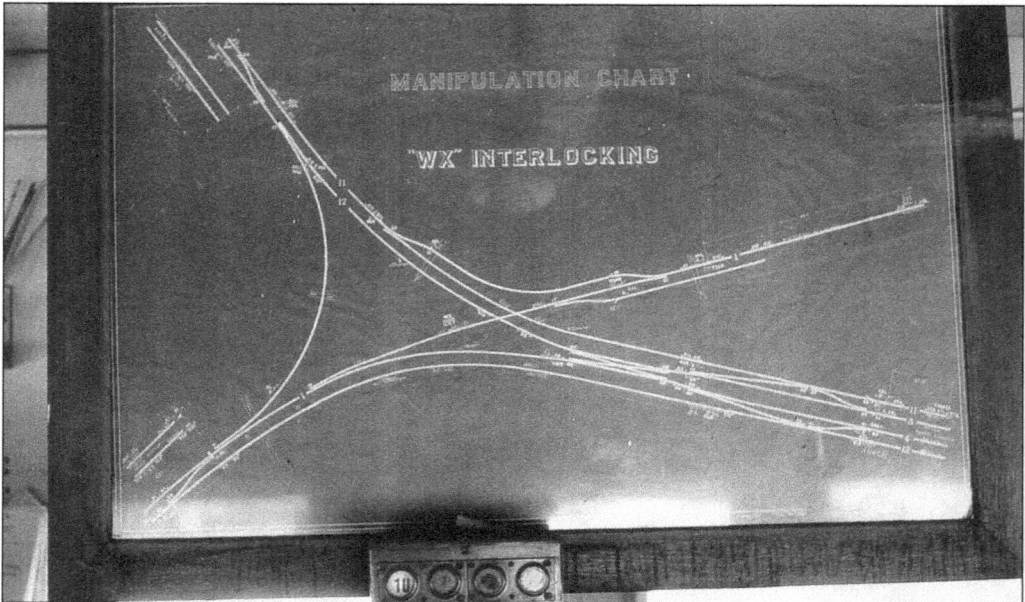

Steam locomotives consumed large quantities of coal and water, so railroads needed en route service facilities to feed these voracious appetites. The B&O coaling facility at Clinton (seen in the photograph above) sat over the mainline tracks. Steam locomotives were gone by the time this photograph was taken, but for a view of a steam engine at this facility, see page 30. A smaller coaling tower served B&O locomotives in Akron (seen in the photograph below). This tower, which still stands, was located in Hill Yard on the Chicago line, but was easily accessible to Valley line trains. A westbound freight gets going in this March 1954 view taken near Arlington Street. The caboose is at the end of a string of coal cars at the coaling tower. (Photographs by Bob Redmond.)

Railroads once built palatial stations, particularly in large cities, but modern stations are far more unpretentious. The Cuyahoga Valley Scenic Railroad station (seen in the photograph above) may look like a traditional depot, but it is actually an open-air shelter, even though the end walls make it appear otherwise. The station is located at the site of the former B&O Howard Street station. Akron's Amtrak station (seen in the photograph below) was a modular building installed in 1998, near Quaker Square and the 1950 Akron Union Depot, with $97,500 funding from the city and $12,500 from the Ohio Rail Development Commission. It was Akron's second Amtrak station, the first having been a trailer located on the same site between 1990 and 1995. Amtrak ceased serving Akron in March 2005, and this station is no longer used. (Photographs by Craig Sanders.)

Two

BALTIMORE AND OHIO

The B&O featured Akron's most extensive freight and passenger operations. Chicago line passenger trains used Union Depot and Hill Yard. Valley line freight trains used Valley Yard and Hazel Street Yard, while passenger trains used Howard Street station.

The Chicago line had 14 passenger trains in the mid-1940s serving New York, Philadelphia, Baltimore, Washington, Pittsburgh, Detroit, and Chicago. By 1960, service had shrunk to eight trains. The *Ambassador*, a Detroit train, combined with the *Capitol Limited* on October 29, 1961. The *Chicago Express* and eastbound *Diplomat* ended November 5, 1967, and the westbound *Diplomat* and eastbound *Gateway* ended west of Akron in January 1970. Akron's last pre-Amtrak passenger trains, the Chicago–Washington *Capitol Limited* and Akron–Washington *Shenandoah*, ended May 1, 1971.

On the Valley line, B&O and the Pennsylvania Railroad operated a joint passenger train to Marietta, which ended in 1932. B&O passenger service to Valley Junction ended in 1935. The last south end service was a Cleveland–Wheeling train that ended September 29, 1951. Cleveland–Baltimore through sleepers had interchanged with Chicago line trains at Akron Junction for many years before B&O began a through train, the *Cleveland Night Express*, on May 24, 1942. Dieselized in September 1951, the *Cleveland Night Express*, by 1962, averaged 30 passengers a day between Cleveland and Washington, and B&O expected to save $300,000 annually by ending it. Nos. 17 and 18 began their final trips on January 4, 1963, having shrunk to a baggage-lounge car, coach, and sleeper.

The financially troubled B&O merged with Chesapeake and Ohio Railway on February 4, 1963. The Chesapeake and Ohio Railway, B&O, and the Western Maryland Railroad became subsidiaries of the Chessie System on June 15, 1973. Seaboard Coast Line Industries, owner of Family Lines System, and the Chessie System merged on November 1, 1980, creating a holding company known as CSX Corporation. The corporate existence of B&O and the Chesapeake and Ohio Railway ended in 1987.

The Chicago line remains Akron's busiest rail line today and carries a diverse mix of traffic. The Valley line has no freight service north of Akron. The Wheeling and Lake Erie Railroad (W&LE) handles the business that still exists between Akron Junction and Krumroy Road.

B&O received 30 EM-1 steam locomotives from Baldwin in 1944–1945. The railroad wanted diesel locomotives but wound up with steam engines due to War Production Board restrictions. These 2-8-8-0 behemoths were the largest steam locomotives on the B&O. Originally assigned to the Cumberland Division, following World War II some Yellowstones were assigned to the Pittsburgh Division to haul Lake Erie mineral traffic. Delivered as Nos. 7600–7629, the locomotives were later renumbered 650–679. All had been retired by 1960, the year that No. 660 (shown in the photograph above pulling a coal train in Akron in March 1957) was scrapped. In the photograph below, No. 678 has already refueled at the coaling tower at Clinton, so the trailing 4-8-2 is taking its turn on this July 1957 day. (Photographs by Bob Redmond.)

B&O had 320 Q class 2-8-2 Mikado steam locomotives working all over the system. The hour is late for B&O steam locomotives in May 1957 as Q-4 No. 405 and a sister locomotive work upgrade, near Tallmadge and Home Avenues in Akron. A traffic slump enabled B&O to phase out steam in early 1958. Built in March 1921, No. 405 was formerly No. 4409. (Photograph by Bob Redmond.)

Trains climbed a 1.05 percent grade from Akron Junction to Cuyahoga Falls, the steepest on the Akron Division. B&O opened a low-grade line in 1905 as an alternative to the original Pittsburgh and Western Railroad route via DeForest and Warren. Q-4b No. 451 leads a coal train in September 1957, near BD cabin where the connection from the Valley line joins the Chicago line. (Photograph by Bob Redmond.)

B&O called its S-1 class 2-10-2 steam locomotives Big Sixes because of their size and numbering in the 6000 series. A 1956 renumbering changed steam locomotive numbers to three digits to avoid conflicts with diesels and reduced the Big Sixes to the 500 series. No. 524 and a sister steamer have a manifest freight in hand at Cuyahoga Falls in March 1957. (Photograph by Bob Redmond.)

Speed was important with some types of freight. Such was the case with the B&O fish train, which arrived in Akron on Thursdays in season, carrying fresh seafood from Chesapeake Bay in baggage cars. While this B&O freight leaving Akron is not carrying fresh seafood, No. 4478, a 2-8-2 class Q-4 steamer, is in a hurry. (Photograph by Glenn G. Grabill; courtesy of John B. Corns collection.)

Located in the southwest corner of Summit County, Clinton was a good place to watch trains of the Pennsylvania Railroad and B&O. B&O No. 4479, a Q 2-8-2 class, is pulling a manifest train through Clinton. Traffic through Clinton is not as heavy today, as three railroad companies, CSX Transportation, R. J. Corman Railroad Group, and Ohio Central Railroad System, interchange cars there. (Photograph by Glenn G. Grabill; courtesy of John B. Corns collection.)

The locomotives from this Valley line train are headed to the service facilities near Akron Junction in June 1957. Lead locomotive No. 421, a Q-4 class Mikado, made history on May 17, 1958, when it pulled a fan trip with more than 800 aboard between Cleveland and Holloway, in what was the last steam operation on the B&O. (Photograph by Bob Redmond.)

What a difference a couple of decades makes. In the photograph above, the B&O has lashed together four steam locomotives to pull a 107-car ore train, shown in May 1956 near Bettes Corner (Tallmadge and Home Avenues) in Akron. Two decades later at this same location (seen in the photograph below), the steam locomotives are long gone but four B&O diesels are needed to pull a coal train. The lead diesel, No. 3837, is a GP38. This site long has been a favorite location of Akron area photographers to capture trains on the B&O's Chicago–Pittsburgh line, now owned by CSX Transportation. The track in the foreground is the former Pennsylvania Railroad and has since been removed. (Above, photograph by Bob Redmond; below, photograph by John Beach.)

The B&O's Valley line between Cleveland and Akron was a conduit for coke bound for Cleveland steel mills. Although the route followed the bank of the Cuyahoga River from Willows in the Cleveland suburb of Independence to Akron, it had a gradually ascending southbound grade. A Q class Mikado is helping an Akron-bound train upgrade along Riverview Road, near Peninsula in June 1957 (seen in the photograph above). Note the caboose behind the locomotive. Some 20 years later, Chessie System diesels continue to pull much the same freight. A Western Maryland GP7 heads a train at Peninsula (seen in the photograph below). Freight trains no longer use these tracks, now owned by the National Park Service, but excursion trains carry visitors through Cuyahoga Valley National Park. (Above, photograph by Bob Redmond; below, photograph by Roger Durfee.)

The eastbound *Shenandoah* was the B&O's late overnight train from Chicago to Pittsburgh, running behind the all-Pullman *Capitol Limited* and all-coach *Columbian*. The westbound *Shenandoah* provided daylight service from Pittsburgh to Chicago and had the most convenient connections with elite western railroad trains. The *Shenandoah* originated and terminated at Jersey City, New Jersey. Renamed the *Diplomat* in Fall 1964, No. 7 ended between Akron and Chicago in January 1970 and subsequently was renamed *Shenandoah*. One of the few Chicago line trains to pass through Akron in daylight, the *Shenandoah* received diesels in 1945, but on this November 1952 day, it is hustling through Kent, past the Erie Railroad yard (left) with T-3C class 4-8-2 No. 5591 in charge (seen in the photograph above). The westbound *Shenandoah* catches early morning light at Kent in September 1954 (seen in the photograph below). (Photographs by Bob Redmond.)

It must have pained the crew of steamer No. 5600, a class N-1 4-4-4-4, duplex to play second fiddle to an A-B set of FT diesels in April 1950 on a westbound manifest freight at Akron Junction. No. 5600 was built in the B&O Mount Clare shops in 1937 and scrapped in October 1950. (Photograph by Bob Redmond.)

Although designed as a switch engine, No. 518, an Alco D55a, is performing helper duty for a Valley line train headed south at Kent Street in Akron on the B&O around 1950. The train had just left Hazel Street Yard, which was the B&O's principal interchange point with the AC&Y. (Photograph by Bob Redmond.)

Excursions sponsored by railroad enthusiast organizations boomed after the end of World War II. Giving impetus to these trips was the realization that diesel locomotives were rapidly replacing steam engines. Fans rode behind steam engines while they could. A steam-powered excursion sponsored by the Midwest Chapter of the National Railway Historical Society pauses at Akron Junction before heading toward Uhrichsville in October 1952. (Photograph by Bob Redmond.)

Every railroad had passenger trains whose job was to serve the small towns bypassed by the limiteds and carry mail and express. The head-end heavy *Chicago Express* earned an operating profit through the mid-1960s. No. 9, which ended west of Pittsburgh on November 6, 1967, is shown in happier days at Clinton behind 4-6-4 No. 5350. (Photograph by Glenn G. Grabill; courtesy of John B. Corns collection.)

The November 6, 1967, discontinuance of the westbound *Chicago Express* and eastbound *Diplomat* left Akron with four B&O passenger trains: westbound and eastbound *Capitol Limited*, westbound *Diplomat* (shown leaving Akron), and eastbound *Gateway*. The Interstate Commerce Commission on January 6, 1970, allowed B&O to end the *Diplomat* and *Gateway* service west of Akron. The trains were losing $195,00 a year and averaged less than eight passengers per day. (Photograph by John Beach.)

Cars were added and removed from passenger trains at larger terminals. A B&O switcher is shown shuffling a combine at Akron Union Depot, which had a track for a setout sleeper. Departing patrons could board the sleeper as early as 9:00 p.m., even if it would not be picked up for several hours. Arriving patrons could remain on board until about 8:00 a.m. (Photograph by Bob Farkas.)

In the early 1960s, B&O began applying a sunburst design on the noses of its locomotives. GP30 No. 6906 leads a manifest freight near Akron Junction in 1965. Through the 1970s, the B&O operated 20 manifest trains a day on the Chicago line through Akron. When mineral and grain trains were counted, traffic could zoom to 30 trains on some days. (Photograph by Ben Eubank.)

The Canton turn threads its way through the Goodyear Tire and Rubber complex in East Akron beneath the Akron and Barberton Belt Railroad bridge on October 21, 1978. The rubber plants were an important B&O customer. Rubber latex from South America was unloaded at Baltimore and arrived in Akron by tank car. B&O relied on the Akron and Barberton Belt Railroad to do the switching involving Akron area industries. (Photograph by John Beach.)

The Valley line crossed under the Chicago–Pittsburgh mainline just east of Arlington Street on Akron's east side. Connecting tracks between the two routes diverged from the Valley line just beyond the bridge. Partially visible at left is the two-story yard office that oversaw operations in the nearby yards on both rail lines. Shown is a light engine move on July 17, 1981. (Photograph by Roger Durfee.)

Grain was everywhere following this 1982 derailment in downtown Akron. The first order of business was rebuilding one of the damaged tracks. A crane lifted derailed cars onto the rails and the cars were taken to a nearby yard for inspection. Some cars have already been placed on the rails in this scene from June 13, 1982. (Photograph by Roger Durfee.)

Some things about railroading are timeless, such as having to stop before reaching one's destination. As the engineer of this eastbound Chessie System train waits in the warm cab of B&O GP40 No. 4298, the conductor has trudged through the snow to the telephone box near JO Tower in downtown Akron, to receive instructions from the dispatcher. The date is January 1979. (Photograph by Roger Durfee.)

The B&O and Pennsylvania Railroad shared tracks between Akron Junction and Warwick Tower in Clinton. For more than 30 years, the B&O and successor Chessie System tried to buy the Pennsylvania Railroad's track. The successor to Chessie Systems, CSX Transportation, was finally able to do this on February 6, 1990. A Chessie Sea-Land intermodal train led by B&O GP40 No. 4028 is eastbound at Clinton in April 1984. (Photograph by Marty Surdyk.)

The B&O's Valley line served the Goodyear Zeppelin Corporation hangar at Akron Municipal Airport (photograph above). Completed in November 1929, the hangar was 1,175 feet long, 350 feet wide, and 211 feet high. It was large enough inside that clouds could form and rain could fall. Two airships could be assembled simultaneously. Many of the more than 300 Goodyear-built blimps were assembled in Akron. Viewers of televised sports events are familiar with Goodyear's three blimps, one of which is shown hovering over a CSX Transportation train in Akron on May 27, 1992. The *Spirit of Akron* was a familiar site over Akron skies, but was retired after a crash on October 29, 1999. Its replacement, the *Spirit of Goodyear*, is based at the Wingfoot Lake Airship facility in nearby Suffield. (Above, photograph by John Beach; below, photograph by Roger Durfee.)

Goodrich, Tew and Company opened Akron's first rubber factory in 1871. Among the entrepreneurs getting into the rubber business was Harvey Firestone, a former buggy maker who began his company in a vacant foundry. Chessie System No. 6327 (GP40) leads an automobile rack train past the Firestone complex in August 1988. The track to the left leads to former Pennsylvania Railroad's South Akron yard. (Photograph by Marty Surdyk.)

CSX Transportation now owns the former B&O Chicago line through Akron and it remains the city's busiest railroad. A westbound CSX Transportation manifest freight passes the site of the 1891 Akron Union Depot (left) in November 1996. The wall at left was part of the ramp leading up to Market Street. The bridge in the background is Park Street. (Photograph by Marty Surdyk.)

Three

ERIE

The first railroad built between the Atlantic and the Great Lakes, the Erie Railroad, had an admirable record as an innovator and weathered five receiverships, but could not match the Pennsylvania Railroad or New York Central Railroad between Chicago and New York. Whereas Pennsylvania Railroad and New York Central Railroad passenger trains went the distance in 16 hours, Erie Railroad trains needed 24 hours. So the Erie Railroad offered friendly and courteous crews, excellent meals, and well-maintained equipment, while focusing on intermediate markets. Akron was the largest intermediate city on Erie Railroad's Chicago–New York route.

Intensified truck and highway competition in the 1950s and high eastern terminal expenses delivered a one-two punch that the Erie Railroad tried to overcome by merging with the Delaware, Lackawanna and Western Railroad on October 17, 1960. While the merger exceeded expectations in saving money, management problems and the erosion of its traffic base plagued the Erie Lackawanna Railway.

For decades, the Erie Railroad had fielded three pairs of passenger trains through Akron. The first to go were the *Atlantic Express* and *Pacific Express* in July 1965. The *Erie Limited* had been Erie's flagship train since its June 2, 1929, debut and was renamed *Phoebe Snow* on October 27, 1963. The *Phoebe Snow* began its final runs on November 27, 1966. The Erie Lackawanna Railway's last intercity passenger train, the *Lake Cities*, ended January 7, 1970.

Norfolk and Western Railway gained control of the Erie Lackawanna Railway on April 1, 1968, and its fortunes brightened. The Erie Lackawanna Railway was still hemorrhaging copious amounts of cash due to lost business, an overbuilt physical plant, and high labor costs. After Hurricane Agnes wreaked havoc by washing out tracks in June 1972, Erie Lackawanna Railway declared bankruptcy. Inclusion in the planning process that led to the creation of the Consolidated Rail Corporation (also known as Conrail) gave the beleaguered Erie Lackawanna Railway access to greatly needed federal funds to shore up operations.

The Erie Lackawanna Railway had one of the finest constructed mainlines into Chicago, but Conrail did not want it, and much of it in Indiana and Ohio was abandoned in 1979. Two small segments of the former Erie Railroad have survived in the Akron area. The W&LE serves the former Erie Railroad between Barberton and Rittman, and Kent and Ravenna.

The Erie Railroad's 155 N1 class 2-8-2 Mikados were built by Baldwin between 1911 and 1913. No. 3065 is working on a freight train at Kent in 1951, in a scene that will not be around much longer. In the early 1950s, the Kent yard was often filled with retired steam locomotives that were awaiting a trip to the scrap yard. (Photograph by Bob Redmond.)

Steam locomotives lasted into the early 1950s on the Erie Railroad through Akron because the Kent Division was near the mines that supplied the Erie Railroad with coal. This ensured that scenes, such as this steam-powered manifest freight train at Ravenna Road in Brady Lake around 1948, would continue. In February 1950, the Erie Railroad awarded contracts to double track its mainline between Akron and Kent. (Photograph by Bob Redmond.)

46

These boxy-looking locomotives were among the Erie Railroad's earliest diesels. Built by General Electric in April 1931, No. 25 (right) was the Erie's only M-3 and its last box cab locomotive. No. 22, built in October 1927, was one of just two M-2 diesels on the Erie Railroad roster. Both worked in Akron, but in September 1949, they awaited their fate in the Kent yard. (Photograph by Bob Redmond.)

The Erie Railroad had some of the fastest freight trains that passed through Akron, partly because these trains carried perishable commodities. Private cars owned by Chicago meatpacking houses were a common sight in Erie Railroad freight trains. No. 3325, a 2-8-5 S-2 class steam locomotive, leads a freight train out of Akron. (Photograph by Glenn G. Grabill; courtesy of John B. Corns collection.)

Kent was the site of a large Erie Railroad yard, shops, and division headquarters. It was one of the town's largest employers and dozens lost their jobs when the Kent Division's last steam locomotives began retiring in 1952. On this day, though, steam is still king as No. 3338, a 2-8-4 S-2 class steamer, leads a freight train eastward from Kent. (Photograph by Glenn G. Grabill; courtesy of John B. Corns collection.)

The Erie Railroad purchased few lightweight passenger cars following World War II, preferring to modernize heavyweight cars at its Susquehanna shops. Yet in 1947, just 8.4 percent of Erie Railroad passenger equipment was more than 30 years old, compared with the industry average of 38.2 percent. No. 2926, a 4-6-2 K-5 class steam locomotive, heads a westbound passenger train at Barberton. (Photograph by Glenn G. Grabill; courtesy of John B. Corns collection.)

Diesels began pulling Erie Railroad freights through Akron in 1944, although diesel switchers had been assigned to the city since the mid-1930s. Among the early diesels used by the Erie Railroad for freight service were FA locomotives built by the American Locomotive Company in Schenectady, New York. A westbound freight hustles through southwest Akron in a view taken from the Wilbeth Avenue pedestrian bridge. (Photograph by Joe Farkas.)

The *Midlander* was renamed *Lake Cities* in November 1947, a name previously used for the *Midlander*'s Cleveland and Buffalo sections. The westbound *Lake Cities* departs Akron in October 1958, behind one of the 14 Electro-Motive E8A passenger locomotives that Erie Railroad ordered in 1951. These diesels introduced a new two-tone green livery and completed the assignment of diesel power to Erie Railroad passenger trains through Akron. (Photograph by Bob Redmond.)

For much of the 20th century, the Erie Railroad operated three pairs of passenger trains between Chicago and New York. The Erie Railroad's passenger marketing focused on travel from intermediate cities to Chicago or New York. Akron was the largest intermediate city the Erie Railroad served on its Chicago–New York route. An eastbound mail and express train pauses at the Akron station on a winter day. (Courtesy of J. Gary Dillon collection.)

The November 28, 1966, discontinuance of the *Phoebe Snow* left the *Lake Cities* as the Erie Lackawanna Railway's last intercity passenger train. Traditionally the Erie Railroad's second best Chicago–New York train, by 1970 the *Lake Cities* was losing $2,700 a day due to falling patronage and lost mail traffic. The westbound *Lake Cities* has three days left to live as it departs Akron on January 3, 1970. (Photograph by John Beach.)

Erie Railroad's No. 520, an Alco S-2 switch engine built in June 1949, was the last Erie Railroad locomotive still carrying its original livery and still working in Akron years after the formation of the Erie Lackawanna Railway in 1960. The Erie Lackawanna Railway was nearly 15 years old when No. 520 was captured working in downtown Akron on April 26, 1975. (Photograph by Richard Jacobs.)

The Erie Railroad was one of America's most innovative railroads. It was the first railroad to link the Atlantic seaboard with the Great Lakes, the first to use the telegraph to coordinate train movements, and the first to install a system-wide radio network. The Erie Railroad often advertised its radio capability on the sides of locomotives and cabooses. (Photograph by John Beach.)

One bright spot for the Erie Lackawanna Railway in the early 1970s was piggyback traffic (called pigs), which accounted for $46 million, nearly 20 percent of the total 1973 revenue. Many of those pigs belonged to United Parcel Service, which liked the Erie Lackawanna Railway schedule. Although the Erie Lackawanna Railway aggressively sought additional intermodal business, it missed out on an estimated $17 million in intermodal revenue in 1973, due to shortages of freight cars and trailers. The Erie Lackawanna Railway piggyback trains, such as this one pausing in Akron on May 9, 1976, in the photograph above, traveled nearly 50 mph behind high horsepower diesel locomotives. In the photograph at left, a Pennsylvania and New York Central Transportation (known as Penn Central Transportation Company) crew watches as an Erie Lackawanna Railway intermodal train passes on an adjacent track in downtown Akron, by the Erie freight station (at right). (Above, photograph by John Beach; left, photograph by Roger Durfee.)

An eastbound Erie Lackawanna Railway freight train passes the yard offices at McCoy Yard in January 1972 (top photograph). The complex was a series of yards including X Yard, Main Yard, and Belt Yard. The latter served the B. F. Goodrich plant. In the bottom photograph, a westbound train passes the far west end of McCoy Yard as the downtown Akron skyline looms on June 8, 1976. The Erie Lackawanna Railway has been part of Conrail for two months, but change is coming. Conrail ceased using most of the Erie Lackawanna mainline in Indiana in September 1977, ending use of the former Erie Railroad as a through-route between Chicago and the East. Conrail also began phasing out McCoy Yard in favor of the former Pennsylvania Railroad South Akron Yard. (Above, photograph by Richard Jacobs; below, photograph by John Beach.)

The industries of Akron and Youngstown provided the Erie Railroad with a substantial amount of freight traffic on its Chicago–East Coast route. Four of the nation's five largest rubber companies had headquarters and manufacturing facilities in Akron. The city also hosted factories manufacturing food products, metals, chemicals, and plastics. Akron rail traffic dropped precipitously in the 1970s, as the tire factories and other manufacturers closed, scaled back operations, or moved production elsewhere. In the photograph above, an RS-3 pulls a cut of cars in McCoy Yard in March 1976. Note the bug-eye marker lamps. In the photograph below, switcher 408, an NW2 built in January 1948 by the Electro-Motive Division of General Motors, backs onto a train on the Erie Lackawanna mainline in Akron. (Above, photograph by Richard Jacobs; below, photograph by Roger Durfee.)

The Erie Railroad began assigning diesel locomotives to its passenger trains serving Akron in July 1947. After the Erie Lackawanna Railway ended intercity passenger service in January 1970, it reassigned its E8A passenger locomotives to freight duty. Three E8As are shown in the photograph above, leading a manifest freight train into McCoy Yard in Akron on April 16, 1976. In the photograph below, a trio of former passenger locomotives eases a manifest freight train past the Erie Railroad passenger station in Akron. This view was taken from the concourse of Akron Union Depot. Stairways from this concourse led to the platform. The concourse leading from the Erie Railroad station waiting room is visible at upper right. The bridge over the tracks in the background is Exchange Street. (Above, photograph by John Beach; below, photograph by Bob Farkas.)

Although the SDP45 locomotive was designed as a passenger locomotive, the Erie Lackawanna Railway bought 34 of them for freight service. The long frame enabled installation of larger fuel tanks, which meant these locomotives could pull freight trains between Chicago and the East Coast without having to refuel. No. 3652, built in June 1969, leads a westbound freight train under Thornton Street in Akron, in March 1976. (Photograph by Richard Jacobs.)

After becoming part of Conrail on April 1, 1976, the former Erie Lackawanna Railway operated much as it had before the merger for more than a year. Conrail applied a diamond-shaped interim logo to noses of the Erie Lackawanna Railway locomotives, as shown by the lead unit of this westbound train passing the Brown-Graves Company lumber mill in Akron. (Courtesy of Akron Railroad Club collection.)

Steam locomotives had disappeared from Akron-area railroads by the late 1950s, but steam-powered excursion trains helped to keep the past alive and to enthrall another generation of railroad enthusiasts. Former Reading Railroad 4-8-4 No. 2102 is steaming up at Kent to pull an excursion train over the former Erie Lackawanna Railway mainline to Pennsylvania in May 1977. (Photograph by Richard Jacobs.)

What happens when two trains try to occupy the same track at the same time? No. 3660 was at the head of a stopped westbound freight train on the mainline, while No. 3324 was sitting in the yard at Kent. No. 3324 inexplicably began rolling on its own, struck the train on the mainline, and derailed. No one was injured in this mishap. (Courtesy of Akron Railroad Club collection.)

Lighted signals at RU Tower in Sterling still guard the crossing of the B&O and Erie Lackawanna Railway, 25 miles west of Akron on May 11, 1985, even though there is no chance of a collision. Conrail pulled up the former Erie Railroad tracks between Burbank and Rittman in the spring of 1983, but this intermediate section of track at Sterling was not removed immediately. Chessie System employees began operating RU Tower in January 1981. The tower closed in 1989. In the photograph below, a crane lifts the rails of the former Erie Railroad track in Akron on September 2, 1980, just south of the Interstate 76 overpass. The rails will be placed on a rail train and, after reconditioning, used elsewhere on Conrail. (Above, photograph by Edward Ribinskas; left, photograph by Roger Durfee.)

Four

PENNSYLVANIA

Akron's first railroad was the first to be dismembered. Best known by its former name of Cleveland, Akron and Columbus Railway, it was the Pennsylvania Railroad's most direct Cleveland–Columbus route, although it meandered through bucolic countryside and over a 1.25 percent grade at Baddow Pass. The Pennsylvania Railroad ran a daily Cleveland–Columbus freight train that conveyed automobile parts manufactured in Bedford and Twinsburg.

The Akron branch also connected Cleveland with the Pennsylvania Railroad's Chicago–Pittsburgh mainline at Orrville, via the Cleveland, Akron and Columbus Railway, or at Massillon (via the former Massillon and Cleveland Railroad, which diverged at Warwick Tower in Clinton). The Massillon and Cleveland Railroad was completed in May 1869 and paralleled B&O's Dover branch. The Pennsylvania Railroad and B&O negotiated a shared trackage arrangement with directional running.

Cleveland-Akron-Columbus Railway (CA&C) passenger service ended December 14, 1950. "To many of us who have known the CA&C all our lives, there is a deep sentimental attachment to the old road," the Akron Railroad Club's *Bulletin* observed. "We are going to miss the rides along the Killibuck Creek and the Kokosing River. We will often think about the stops at the little villages, the glaciated and rugged country around Glenmount, and the climb to Baddow Pass."

The Pennsylvania Railroad operated an Akron–Hudson shuttle that connected with Cleveland–Pittsburgh passenger trains. The shuttle, which used self-propelled cars dubbed doodlebugs, made its final trips on July 31, 1951, leaving the Akron–New York *Akronite* as Akron's last Pennsylvania Railroad passenger train. Reduced to an Akron–Hudson connecting train on April 26, 1953, the *Akronite* ended April 26, 1958.

The Pennsylvania Railroad and New York Central Railroad merged on February 1, 1968, to form Penn Central Transportation Company, which favored the New York Central Railroad's Cleveland–Columbus route. Flooding on July 4, 1969, severed the former Cleveland, Akron and Columbus Railway north of Holmesville. It was never reestablished as an Akron–Columbus route. The Clinton–Orrville segment was abandoned in 1986, except for a short segment used as an industrial spur in Orrville.

Abandoned between Akron Junction and Cuyahoga Falls in the early 1990s, the Interstate Commerce Commission approved abandonment between Hudson and Cuyahoga Falls on November 10, 1994. The track was sold in 1995 to the Summit County Port Authority for possible commuter train use.

The Pennsylvania Railroad had diverging routes at Warwick (Clinton). The former Cleveland, Akron and Columbus Railway angled southwestward toward Columbus, while the former Massillon and Cleveland Railroad ran southward to Massillon parallel to the B&O's Dover line. A Pennsylvania Railroad manifest freight train behind an M-1 steam locomotive crosses the Dover line, the former Cleveland, Lorain and Wheeling Railroad, in the late 1940s. (Photograph by Bob Redmond.)

In an effort to cut the costs of providing passenger service on lightly patronized routes, many railroads turned to self-propelled cars powered by gasoline or diesel fuel. Affectionately nicknamed doodlebugs, the cars were designed to run solo, but could be operated in pairs. The Pennsylvania Railroad assigned doodlebugs to its Akron–Hudson shuttle trains and to one pair of Akron–Columbus trains. (Courtesy of Cuyahoga Falls Public Library.)

The *Akronite* was among the 28 premier Pennsylvania Railroad passenger trains designated as the Blue Ribbon fleet. It carried sleepers, coaches, and a diner-lounge between Akron and New York. Reduced in 1953 to an Akron–Hudson train connecting with the Cleveland–New York *Clevelander*, the inbound *Akronite* still had a New York through-sleeper as it arrived at Cuyahoga Falls in July 1956 behind Alco RS-3 No. 8910. (Photograph by H. Vaughn Smith.)

The busiest Pennsylvania Railroad line in Summit County was the Cleveland–Pittsburgh route that passed through Hudson. In the early 1940s, this route hosted 36 passenger and 60 freight trains a day. The Pennsylvania Railroad had two pairs of Cleveland–Pittsburgh trains, the *Morning Steeler* and *Afternoon Steeler*. The Steeler is shown at Earlville in the early 1950s. (Photograph by Bob Redmond.)

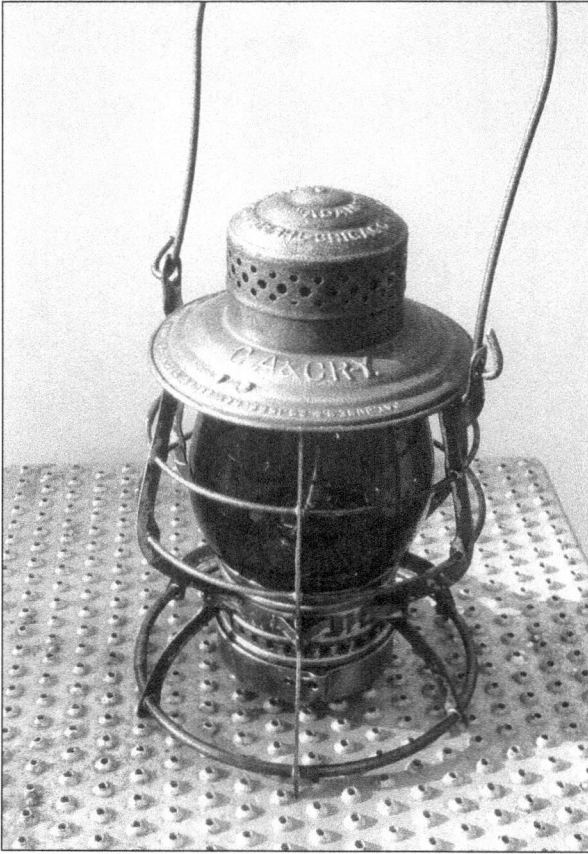

Railroad employees used lanterns to communicate as well as to see. Railroads typically placed their names or initials on the lanterns, including the globes. The advent of radio communication largely replaced the use of lanterns for communication, but they are still used for illumination. This lantern was originally used on the Pennsylvania Railroad predecessor Cleveland, Akron and Columbus Railway. (Courtesy of Paul Vernier collection.)

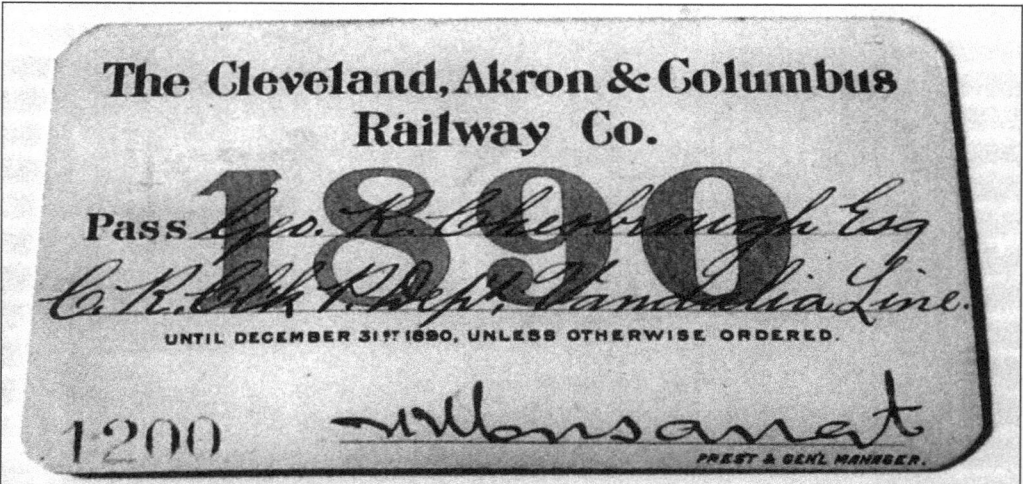

Passes enabled the bearer to ride free on the passenger trains of the issuing railroad. Passes were typically carried by railroad executives, employees, and selected guests. It was commonplace for some railroads to issue passes to retired employees. This pass was issued in 1890 by the Cleveland, Akron and Columbus Railway Company, which later was absorbed by the Pennsylvania Railroad. (Courtesy of Paul Vernier collection.)

Early Pennsylvania Railroad diesels, particularly passenger locomotives, featured an attractive livery of gold pinstripes overlaid on Tuscan red. This was later modified to a solid stripe and by the late 1960s, Pennsylvania Railroad locomotives carried merely the Pennsylvania Keystone. In the photograph above, Pennsylvania Railroad SD45 No. 6217 shows the minimalist livery as it leads a freight train at Wilbeth Road in southwestern Akron. This 3,600-horsepower, six-axle locomotive was built by the Electro-Motive Division of General Motors in 1968. The "SD" denoted "special duty." In the photograph below, switcher 9115, a DS 4-4-6 built by Baldwin in 1948, leads a local freight train past the Erie Lackawanna Railway passenger station in Akron. (Photographs by Bob Farkas.)

Nothing was finer, so it was said, than dinner in the diner. These former Pennsylvania Railroad Pullman cars were converted to a stationary diner by a Hudson restaurateur. Shown on August 30, 1970, they occupied a former railroad right-of-way. The line was rerouted in 1905 to create an air line without grade crossings between Hudson and Ravenna. (Photograph by Robert MacCallum.)

The Pennsylvania Railroad ordered 200 FP20 locomotives from Fairbanks Morse between 1947 and 1956. The locomotives were rated at 2,000 horsepower. No. 9473 is in command of a westbound freight west of downtown Akron in January 1957, as it passes the Erie Railroad yard. At one time, the Pennsylvania Railroad operated 14 freight trains a day on its Akron route. (Photograph by Bob Redmond.)

The Pennsylvania and New York Central Railroads began discussing a merger in September 1957. Fierce competitors in the East and Midwest, the Pennsylvania and New York Central Railroads were the nation's first and second largest railroads. It was a disastrous merger, and Penn Central Transportation Company (the result of the merger) entered bankruptcy in June 1970. The fireman of a Pennsylvania Railroad FP7A checks his train before leaving South Akron Yard on October 7, 1962. (Photograph by John Beach.)

Penn Central Transportation Company rolling stock carried an interlocking P and C that some wags called the mating worms. Originally the P was red and the C was white, as shown on this F unit passing the Erie Lackawanna Railway passenger station in Akron, but this soon gave way to an all-white PC herald. Penn Central freight cars and cabooses were painted green. (Photograph by Bob Farkas.)

Penn Central Transportation Company inherited hundreds of locomotives from its predecessor companies and repainted them into a utilitarian black livery with white lettering. F7A No. 1725 is leading three sister units on the former Pennsylvania Railroad, west of downtown Akron. The bridge in the background is Thornton Street, which spanned the tracks of the Pennsylvania, B&O, and Erie Railroads. (Photograph by Richard Jacobs.)

Although built as an Akron–Columbus route, the Pennsylvania Railroad, Penn Central, and Conrail used the line for through trains between Cleveland and the Chicago–Pittsburgh mainline at Orrville or Massillon. The Pennsylvania Railroad shared a double-track line with the B&O between Clinton and Massillon. The former Pennsylvania Railroad portion of this route was removed in 1987. Train MC-97 passes through Barberton in April 1977. (Photograph by Roger Durfee.)

The former Cleveland, Akron and Columbus Railway featured backwoods railroading at its best. A crew member would throw a newspaper for an elderly farmer, whose sheep dog delivered it to his master. Penn Central reduced service to a daily local freight, shown arriving at Clinton in September 1976, behind Penn Central GP9 No. 7047 (seen in the photograph above). Conrail took over the Akron branch on April 1, 1976, and locomotives from various railroads soon appeared, including Lehigh Valley Railroad No. 626, which was an Alco C628 shown on the line to Columbus at Warwick Tower (seen in the photograph below). Traffic diminished in the 1980s and the Clinton–Orrville segment was abandoned in 1986. Conrail offered its Akron lines for sale in March 1991, and four years later, the Summit County Port Authority purchased the track between Hudson and Cuyahoga Falls for possible commuter train use. (Photographs by Roger Durfee.)

At 5:58 p.m. on July 31, 1940, an Akron-bound gasoline-electric car collided with a northbound freight train in Cuyahoga Falls. The engineer, conductor, and another railroad employee jumped before the collision and survived, but 43 others died, including the baggage man. Investigators concluded that the passenger train engineer may have blacked out and thus failed to stop in Silver Lake for a meet with the freight train. He came to just over a mile beyond the meeting point, but too late to avert the collision. The coroner ruled that nine of the dead had died on impact, while the others burned to death after the gasoline tank ruptured and ignited. Rescue workers remove the victims (seen in the photograph above), while the photograph below shows the car wedged against the lead freight train steam locomotive. (Courtesy of Pennsylvania Railroad Technical and Historical Society.)

Cuyahoga Falls seventh-graders Joseph Gajovski, Nathan Gera, and Clarissa Melvin launched a class project to create a memorial to the 43 victims of the 1940 passenger train accident in Cuyahoga Falls. The memorial was dedicated July 31, 2005, the 65th anniversary of the accident. In the photograph at right, Cuyahoga Falls mayor Don Robart (right) along with Melvin (left) and Gajovski (center) lift a sheet to reveal the monument. Family members and friends who lost loved ones in the accident were invited to the dedication ceremony. In the photograph below, Olga Fisher holds a photograph of her sister Mary Badonsky, an Akron resident who died in the accident at age 25. The collision, which occurred behind and to the left of the monument, was the worst railroad disaster in Akron-area history. (Photographs by Craig Sanders.)

The Pennsylvania Railroad's Akron branch joined the Cleveland–Pittsburgh mainline at Hudson in northeast Summit County. In the latter years, Conrail trains serving Akron came out of Motor Yard in Macedonia. The crew would go on duty at South Akron Yard and be transported to Motor Yard to catch their train. In the photograph above, the Akron local pauses at Hudson in 1987 behind Conrail No. 3285, a GP40-2. An operator in the Hudson station (visible behind the locomotive) controlled the switches and signals here with the centralized traffic control panel shown in the photograph below. The Cleveland–Pittsburgh line had block signals, but the Akron branch was dark territory, and the operator had to hand up train orders to trains using the branch. Conrail ceased using the Akron branch in 1994. (Photographs by Richard Antibus.)

Five

AKRON, CANTON AND YOUNGSTOWN

The Cleveland, St. Louis and Delphos Railroad built a narrow-gauge line in 1881 between Delphos and Carey in western Ohio, but financial troubles put it into the hands of the Ohio Railway, which had formed November 10, 1883. Renamed Pittsburg, Akron and Western Railroad in 1890, a Carey–Akron route was completed January 24, 1891. The company was renamed Northern Ohio Railway on August 14, 1895.

The Pittsburg, Akron and Western Railroad wanted to connect with the Pittsburgh and Western Railroad in Akron, but this fell through when the B&O leased the Pittsburgh and Western Railroad in early 1891. The Pittsburg, Akron and Western Railroad eyed a connection with the Pittsburgh and Lake Erie Railroad at Youngstown, but dropped the idea after surveying as far as Mogadore. New York Central Railroad subsidiary Lake Erie and Western leased the Northern Ohio Railway on October 1, 1895. The physical condition of the Northern Ohio Railway deteriorated and the top speed fell to 25 mph. Trains did not operate on Sunday or at night.

The AC&Y formed June 6, 1907. Its 9.5-mile Akron–Mogadore route opened October 1, 1912. Plans to build further east were dropped during World War I, but AC&Y leased the Northern Ohio Railway on March 1, 1920. In 1948, AC&Y surveyed a route between Mogadore and Girard, but the expansion never occurred and the AC&Y never served Canton or Youngstown.

In 1920, the AC&Y purchased three motorcars for passenger service, operating 14 trips a day. The motorcar trains ended in 1922, leaving a pair of Akron-Delphos mixed trains inherited from the Northern Ohio Railway as the last passenger service. AC&Y had the only open platform coach still operating in Ohio and the state's last mixed trains. Patronage was minimal, and the trains survived because of mail revenue. The mail contract ended in October 1950, and the mixed trains, affectionately known as the Delphos Bullet, made their final trips July 20, 1951.

Norfolk and Western Railway acquired the AC&Y on October 15, 1964, although it continued a paper existence through 1982. Norfolk Southern Corporation, the successor to the Norfolk and Western Railway, sold the former AC&Y to the W&LE in May 1990.

No. 320 was a 2-8-0 class M built by Baldwin in 1922 and retired in 1952. It is shown near Brittain Yard in Akron with a manifest freight. The three hopper cars may hold bituminous coal, which since 1912 had been the number one commodity hauled by the AC&Y, although virtually none of it originated on line. (Photograph by Glenn G. Grabill; courtesy of John B. Corns collection.)

AC&Y serviced its locomotives at Brittain Yard in East Akron, where it had a roundhouse and turntable. No. 402, shown next to the turntable in the late 1940s, was built by Lima Locomotive Works in 1928. The class R 2-8-2 remained on the AC&Y roster until 1955. It was subsequently scrapped. (Photograph by Bob Redmond.)

A freight train waits in the siding while the AC&Y mixed train does some work on January 2, 1950. Steam locomotive No. 322 is a Baldwin class M 2-8-0 built in 1923 and scrapped after its retirement in 1950. The man on the ground talking with the engineer is Akron Railroad Club member Bruce Triplett. (Photograph by Bob Redmond.)

Ohio Edison Company hired an AC&Y work train to help build a transmission line in March 1950 along the railroad right-of-way in East Akron. The train is shown at Beech Street putting up the electric line. The steam locomotive is a Baldwin M class 2-8-0 built in 1922 and scrapped after retirement in 1952. (Photograph by Walter Long; courtesy of John Schon collection.)

The AC&Y began Akron–Mogadore commuter service on January 4, 1920, using McKeen motorcar No. 51. That spring, AC&Y purchased two General Electric gas-electric cars, Nos. 55 and 56, from the Bangor and Aroostook Railroad to expand service to Copley, probably in July. The service was lightly patronized and discontinued in December 1921. A Texas railroad bought Nos. 55 and 56 in 1922. (Courtesy of James Spangler collection.)

A banner was the only fanfare when the AC&Y carried passengers for the final time on July 20, 1951. The Delphos Bullet was a sarcastic moniker given the mixed trains, which were scheduled to travel the 162 miles between Akron and Delphos in eight hours. In 1950, the last mixed trains in Ohio carried 1,049 passengers and earned $975. (Courtesy of John Wunderle collection.)

The square AC&Y herald was used from the 1920s through World War II. It featured white interlocking A, C, and Y figures on a red background. As shown on M class 2-8-0 No. 321, the logo was centered on the tender. No. 321 was among the first two Consolidations built by Baldwin for the AC&Y in 1922. It was retired and scrapped in 1951. (Courtesy of H. Vaughn Smith collection.)

No. 355 was an Alco class O 2-8-0 built in 1903 for the Cleveland, Columbus, Cincinnati and Indianapolis Railway (Big Four). Acquired in 1929 and retired in 1950, it is shown at Brittain Yard. The AC&Y continued to purchase steam motive power through 1947, including the purchase of a class R-2 locomotive built by Lima in 1944. AC&Y retired the last of its steam locomotives in 1955. (Photograph by Bob Redmond.)

The first AC&Y diesels arrived in 1942 and were used as switch engines. In September 1947, AC&Y signed a contract with Fairbanks-Morse for four road diesels. The first of these class D-2 units arrived in January 1948. AC&Y eventually owned 18 F-M locomotives, the last of which was purchased in March 1957. All were painted chromium-yellow with black and silver highlights. In the photograph above, two F-M road switchers pull a manifest freight near Brittain Yard on September 28, 1963. A solo unit pulls a train west of Akron in the photograph below. Manufactured goods and mine products accounted for 90 percent of AC&Y's freight business in 1962. Only 9 percent of the freight hauled originated on the AC&Y, reflecting its role as a bridge carrier. (Above, photograph by John Beach; below, courtesy of Richard Jacobs collection.)

Although railroads go to great lengths to ensure that their trains stay on track, derailments are inevitable. That is why one often finds a crane, such as this one owned by the AC&Y, in a corner of many railroad yards. The AC&Y acquired the X-991 in 1935 as a replacement for a smaller crane (X-990) that had been built in 1899. (Photograph by Richard Jacobs.)

Old passenger train equipment does not die; it frequently turns up in work train service. The AC&Y had little use for these cars after it ceased hauling mail on October 31, 1950, and express the following year. Shown are a baggage car (far left) and a baggage-mail car in Brittain Yard in Akron in May 1971, two decades after passenger service ended. (Photograph by Richard Jacobs.)

Construction of Brittain Yard began in 1916. Although the roundhouse, which once had 11 stalls, and the coaling tower were razed in the early 1970s, the turntable has survived. After Norfolk and Western Railway acquired the AC&Y in 1964, it assigned to it a fleet of GP-7 and GP-9 locomotives, many of them of Nickel Plate Road heritage. (Photograph by Roger Durfee.)

The original River Styx Road trestle near Medina was completed on December 16, 1890, and was the second longest on the AC&Y at 900 feet. It was over 85 feet high. It was replaced in 1925. The trestle can be seen by motorists on nearby Interstate 71 during winter months. A Norfolk and Western Railway freight train crosses the trestle on March 14, 1981. (Photograph by Roger Durfee.)

78

The AC&Y was short of cabooses after acquiring the Northern Ohio Railway in 1920, so 11 matchbox cabooses were built at the Brittain Yard shops from sturdy (but obsolete) wooden boxcars built in 1912. No. 54, converted in 1923, served until July 1965. Seven of the cars had bay windows and are thought to be the first bay window cabooses in the United States. (Courtesy of Richard Jacobs collection.)

To commemorate the AC&Y, the W&LE gave GP35 No. 107 an AC&Y herald and lettering. The locomotive is shown pulling a passenger special on August 2, 2003, which carried dignitaries and guests to the rededication ceremony of the AC&Y depot in Copley. The depot, built in 1891, was moved from its original site and converted into a museum. (Photograph by Richard Jacobs.)

The second coming of the W&LE occurred in 1990 when Norfolk Southern sold 575.8 miles of track, including the former AC&Y, to the Wheeling Acquisition Corporation for more than $40 million. Although the AC&Y between Carey and Delphos was abandoned in 1982, today's operations on the former AC&Y have much in common with its ancestor. Stone remains a principle commodity carried over the route. In the photograph above, the W&LE interchanges a stone train with CSX Transportation at the AC&Y transfer north of downtown Akron. This was a longtime transfer point between the AC&Y and the Erie, Pennsylvania, and B&O Railroads. In the photograph below, a W&LE stone train makes its way over a trestle in downtown Akron on May 1, 2005. (Above, photograph by Roger Durfee; below, photograph by Peter Bowler.)

Six

WHEELING AND LAKE ERIE

There have been two incarnations of the W&LE. The earliest ancestor of the original W&LE was the Carroll County Railroad, a 10-mile, horse-drawn operation that began May 24, 1853, between Carrollton and Oneida. This road eventually evolved into a Cleveland–Zanesville narrow-gauge route that reached Mogadore in January 1881, Kent in May 1881, and Bedford on July 4, 1881. Cleveland passenger service began February 21, 1882.

Many Cleveland industries switched from coal to oil for their furnaces and boilers in the late 1880s, hindering the financial performance of the Tip-Top Route. Acquired by the W&LE on August 5, 1899, the one-time Connotton Valley Railway crossed the W&LE's Toledo–Wheeling, West Virginia, line at Harmon. Passenger service had begun between Cleveland and Wheeling by October 1899. This would be W&LE's last passenger service, with Nos. 32 and 35 making their final trips on July 17, 1938.

Seeking access to the mid-Atlantic region, the Nickel Plate Road leased the W&LE on December 1, 1949, in a deal that included the Pittsburgh and West Virginia Railway line to Pittsburgh. The Nickel Plate Road merged with Norfolk and Western Railway on October 16, 1964. The Norfolk and Western Railway merged with the Southern Railway on June 1, 1982, and both became subsidiaries of Norfolk Southern Corporation.

As part of a program to sell underperforming, marginal, or unprofitable branch lines, Norfolk Southern Corporation, in May 1990, sold the former W&LE between Cleveland and Harmon to a newly constituted W&LE. Norfolk Southern Corporation had sold the Harmon–Zanesville segment on April 16, 1988, to Jerry Jacobson, who renamed it Ohio Central Railroad System.

Like the original W&LE, the modern Wheeling was a coal-hauling railroad. But when that business began drying up in the 1990s, a new management team headed by Larry Parsons was brought in on April 1, 1992, and diversified the traffic base. Parsons and many of his top managers once worked at the Denver and Rio Grande Western Railroad, and Wheeling locomotives were lettered in a style reminiscent of Denver and Rio Grande Western Railroad speed lettering. Today's Wheeling serves a territory stretching from Cleveland and Toledo to Pittsburgh and Wheeling. The W&LE has the most Akron area freight customers.

On August 2, 1911, W&LE 4-4-0 No. 350, with passenger train No. 32, rushed into a passing siding at Twinsburg, striking the rear of freight train No. 194. The caboose was lifted off its frame and thrown over the locomotive's boiler. Conductor G. I. Gordy and flagman Frank B. Tressel were in the cupola at the moment of impact, but, remarkably, neither was injured. (Courtesy of John B. Corns collection.)

In a scene most typical of the W&LE, I-2 class 2-6-6-2 No. 8419 lumbers through Harmon in 1933 with a westbound coal train from Pine Valley. Of its two classes of Mallets, W&LE preferred the I-2 because of its higher tractive effort (8,000 pounds more than the I-3) and greater track speeds afforded by larger, 63-inch drivers. (Courtesy of John B. Corns collection.)

The W&LE was better known for hauling coal than passengers. Some W&LE passenger trains featured diners and parlor cars, but patronage peaked in 1911, and revenue began to decline. W&LE passenger service ended July 17, 1938, when Nos. 32 and 35 made their final trips between Cleveland and Wheeling. The last run of No. 32 has just left the depot at Mogadore. (Courtesy of John B. Corns collection.)

The Nickel Plate Road maintained steam locomotive power on the former W&LE through 1957, although most of it was concentrated east and south of Brewster. However, some steam power continued to ply the Cleveland line into the late 1950s, including the S-4 class No. 803. It is shown at the yard in Kent about to leave with a manifest freight. (Photograph by Bob Redmond.)

The Kent yard was a good place to see steam locomotives in the 1950s. No. 958, was an H-5a class 2-8-2 built by Brooks in August 1917. No. 708 (left) was an S class 2-8-4 built by Schenectady in October 1934. Both locomotives were sold for scrap with the 958 retired on December 20, 1956, and the 708 on April 22, 1961. (Photograph by Robert Rohal.)

Engine crews were willing to strike a pose in the cab if someone with a camera happened to come by. No. 814, shown in the yard at Kent, was an S-4 class 2-8-4 locomotive built by Schenectady in January 1939. It was sold for scrap in December 1963. (Photograph by Robert Rohal.)

Railroaders spend a fair amount of time sitting still. This Nickel Plate Road crew is passing time at the Kent depot waiting for its next assignment to arrive. During the 1950s, when this photograph was taken, the former Connotton Valley Railway enjoyed renewed prosperity due to the Nickel Plate Road having developed 700 acres near Solon that attracted six large industries in six years. (Photograph by Robert Rohal.)

Working for the railroad was usually a good job to have in many American communities during the early 20th century. The work was steady, and the pay was good, even if the hours were unpredictable. A Nickel Plate Road crew is shown switching cars at Kent. No. 429 is a GP7, that was built in July 1953 and retired on July 31, 1980. (Photograph by Robert Rohal.)

Railroad enthusiasts and some railroad employees lamented the replacement of steam locomotives with diesels, but railroad management liked diesels because they were generally less costly to operate than steam engines. A pair of Alco S-4 switchers, built for the Nickel Plate Road in June 1953, are working in the yard at Kent. No. 81 retired in March 1975, and No. 82 retired in May 1973. (Photograph by Robert Rohal.)

CSX Transportation may haul the most freight through Akron, but the modern W&LE has the most freight customers in Akron. Two W&LE trains meet at Mogadore, where the AC&Y interchanged with the original W&LE, on February 13, 2001. A former Denver and Rio Grande Western Railroad locomotive leads one of the trains. (Photograph by Roger Durfee.)

Seven

AKRON AND
BARBERTON BELT

Among the many legacies of Akron industrialist Ohio Columbus Barber, who founded Barberton and owned the Diamond Match Company, is the Akron and Barberton Belt Railroad (A&BB). It opened July 12, 1892, between Barberton and Akron, and Barber talked of expanding to Cleveland and Youngstown. The A&BB never advanced beyond Summit County.

Growing industrialization in Barberton and Akron boosted the A&BB's fortunes, which attracted the attention of Akron's other railroads. Representatives from the Pennsylvania, B&O, Erie, and Northern Ohio Railroads met with Barber on May 7, 1902. Pennsylvania Railroad vice president James McCrea asked Barber to name a selling price. Barber responded that his railroad was not for sale. After further discussion, McCrea offered $500,000, which Barber promptly rejected. After conferring with an associate, Barber stated a price of $2 million. Six days later, he sold the A&BB for $1 million. The new owners bonded the A&BB at $3 million, prompting Barber to think he had been swindled out of $2 million. He spent the rest of his life criticizing railroads and calling for government ownership.

The A&BB was completed between Barberton and East Akron on October 15, 1904, and in 1905, acquired the 2-mile Barberton and Southern Railroad, giving the A&BB a Barberton connection with the Erie and Pennsylvania Railroads. Ownership of the A&BB was a partnership, but the Pennsylvania Railroad oversaw operations. The A&BB owned little rolling stock, just a handful of locomotives, two cabooses, and a flatcar.

The decline of industry in Akron and Barberton took a toll on the A&BB, which lost $988,000 in 1979, suffered 51 derailments, and came close to extinction. A $1.3 million state loan for track and equipment rehabilitation helped cut the derailment rate to zero by 1983. That same year PPG Industries halted most Barberton operations and the A&BB lost 65 percent of its business.

The A&BB was sold for under $2 million in July 1994 to the Akron and Barberton Cluster, a wholly owned subsidiary of the Wheeling Corporation, which owns the W&LE. Much of the Barberton–East Akron route has been abandoned in favor of using CSX Transportation track.

Four railroads shared ownership of the A&BB, but as the managing partner, the Pennsylvania Railroad oversaw operations. That included maintaining the equipment. A&BB No. 5076, a 0-4-0ST, is shown at the Pennsylvania Railroad shops in Canton in 1937. No. 5076 was a class A-3a locomotive. (Photograph by Glenn G. Grabill; courtesy of John B. Corns collection.)

The A&BB purchased 2-6-0 Baldwin Mogul No. 7 in 1913. The last active steam locomotive on the A&BB, No. 7 was last used in the summer of 1947 when a diesel was sidelined. It was sold for scrap in February 1948. No. 7 was known for a pleasant whistle that was similar to that of a passenger locomotive. (Photograph by Glenn G. Grabill; courtesy of John B. Corns collection.)

Much of the steam power on the A&BB is thought to have followed the practices of the Pennsylvania Railroad. No. 17 was built by Baldwin and is strikingly similar to a Pennsylvania Railroad B6sb, aside from the A&BB locomotive having a larger tender. It is probable that locomotives borrowed from all four owning railroads operated on the A&BB on occasion. (Courtesy of H. Vaughn Smith collection.)

The A&BB ordered its first diesel engine in 1942. The A&BB has operated with a wide array of motive power including Alco RS-3 No. 5408, which is shown in Barberton in April 1971. Built in April 1951 for the Pennsylvania Railroad, the A&BB bought it in 1964. Scrapped in 1972, No. 5408 was the only Alco that the A&BB ever owned. (Photograph by Richard Jacobs.)

The A&BB served all of Akron's freight districts. The line began in Barberton and ended in East Akron. The A&BB twisted and turned its way through Akron, crossing 64 streets, many without benefit of grade crossing protection signals, on its 12.6 miles of mainline track. In the photograph above, a train led by SW1200 Nos. 1210 and 1205, leased from Norfolk and Western Railway, has just come from the AC&Y interchange on the other side of the culvert (Martha Avenue) in East Akron and is passing the Goodyear plant in October 1982. Westbound trains faced a stiff grade that tested the mettle of man and machine alike. In the photograph below, an A&BB train passes the Burger Iron Company. (Courtesy of Akron Railroad Club collection.)

Between July 1972 and October 1982, the A&BB operated with an assortment of leased locomotives, many of them supplied by its owner railroads. One of these was Norfolk and Western Railway Alco RS-2 No. 2548, shown switching cars in Barberton in April 1971. Although the decline of heavy industry in Akron and Barberton affected all railroads, the A&BB was hit particularly hard. (Photograph by Richard Jacobs.)

The A&BB locomotives were serviced at an engine house in Barberton. SW1500 No. 1502 was purchased from Conrail in October 1982. The caboose was built for Canadian National Railway and purchased from the Lehigh Valley Railroad in 1962. The only other piece of rolling stock other than a locomotive or caboose the A&BB owned was a flatcar. (Photograph by Dennis Bydash.)

The A&BB may have crossed many streets at grade, but it built bridges over intersecting railroads, including the B&O's line to Canton. Nos. 1501 and 1502 are shown on the bridge over the B&O inside the East Akron complex of the Goodyear Tire and Rubber Company on February 2, 1990. (Photograph by Roger Durfee.)

Much of the A&BB in Akron was abandoned in the early 1990s and removed in 1995. A&BB trains then got around by using trackage rights on other roads, most notably CSX Transportation. By now known as the Akron and Barberton Cluster, one of their trains is seen here on CSX Transportation (former B&O) trackage at Wilbeth Road on July 24, 1999. (Courtesy of Akron Railroad Club collection.)

Eight

OTHER
RAILROAD OPERATIONS

When chartered April 30, 1903, the Lake Erie and Pittsburgh (LE&P) was envisioned as a Youngstown–Lorain line. Two years later the Lake Shore and Michigan Southern Railway—soon to be part of the New York Central System—purchased the LE&P. The New York Central System and Pennsylvania Railroad split construction costs, and the LE&P opened October 15, 1911, between a connection with New York Central System's Cleveland Short line near Marcy and the Pennsy's Cleveland and Pittsburg Railroad line at Brady Lake. The Pennsylvania Railroad, however, did not use the LE&P, which passed through northern Summit County. Most of the LE&P was abandoned soon after the February 1, 1968, formation of Penn Central Transportation Company.

Henry Lucas of the Cuyahoga County Fair and Siegfried Buerling of Hale Farm suggested establishing a steam railroad excursion service in 1967 on the B&O between Cleveland and Akron through Cuyahoga Valley National Park. B&O nixed that idea, but in 1975 the Chessie System approved the excursions, operated by the Cuyahoga Valley Scenic Railroad.

After the Chessie System announced on September 5, 1984, that it would seek abandonment between Akron and Independence, the National Park Service began negotiating to purchase the route. Before the sale was consummated on September 29, 1987, the line had been abandoned between Independence and Akron, and the 1986 and 1987 excursion seasons cancelled. Excursions resumed in 1988. In June 2003, excursions began between Akron and Canton using former Valley Railway line track owned by public agencies in Summit and Stark counties.

Created to take over the nation's intercity rail passenger service, Amtrak bypassed Akron when it began May 1, 1971. The nearest Amtrak station was in Canton. Amtrak reached Akron on November 11, 1990, when the Chicago–New York Broadway Limited was rerouted over CSX Transportation through Akron and Youngstown. A financial crisis that prompted route cutbacks resulted in the Broadway Limited making its final trips September 9 and 10, 1995. Amtrak service resumed in Akron on August 10, 1998, when the Chicago–New York Three Rivers began stopping there. The Three Rivers was discontinued west of Pittsburgh on March 7, 2005, due to low patronage and Amtrak's giving up the mail and express business that had sustained the train.

New York Central trains operating on the LE&P line to Cleveland used the Pennsylvania Railroad between Brady Lake and Ravenna, and the B&O between Ravenna and Youngstown. Eastbound trains descended a grade and ran parallel to the Pennsylvania Railroad tracks (seen in the photograph above) before entering them at Brady Lake Tower. A Mohawk class L 4-8-2 steam locomotive heads a stone train bound for Youngstown in May 1951. Westbound New York Central trains ascended the grade from Brady Lake and crossed over the Pennsylvania Railroad tracks on a bridge visible in the background of the top photograph. In the photograph below, an A-B-A lash-up of F series diesels leads a manifest freight train as it climbs the grade in March 1957. The former LE&P had no grade crossings and crossed creeks and valleys on large trestles. (Photographs by Bob Redmond.)

Shortly after the 1968 creation of Penn Central, trains using the LE&P were rerouted to the Cleveland–Pittsburgh line of the former Pennsylvania Railroad. Within a year of the merger, most of the LE&P was out of service. A local in November 1976 exits the small portion of the LE&P that survived because it served a sand and gravel pit at Hugo near Twin Lakes. (Photograph by Roger Durfee.)

Most large railroads have executive trains for the use of top railroad officials, which are also used to entertain shippers and dignitaries on special occasions. The Conrail executive train heads west near Brady Lake on October 21, 1991. The rear car is a theater car that features a large picture window and angled seating that enables passengers to gain a panoramic view of the railroad. (Photograph by Roger Durfee.)

Hooping up train orders was once a common practice, but this has all but disappeared from railroading. Today train orders are transmitted by fax or given over the radio by the train dispatcher. In February 1978, however, handing up train orders was alive and well at the Conrail block station at South Street in Akron. This block station has since closed. (Photograph by Roger Durfee.)

Although passengers considered the clickity-clack of a train to be romantic, railroad executives heard a rail that was one day closer to needing replacement. Therefore jointed rail gave way to welded rail. A CSX Transportation track worker is using a process known as thermo-welding to rejoin two rails that had pulled apart during cold weather in Akron on February 12, 1995. (Photograph by Roger Durfee.)

Regional railroad, R. J. Corman Railroad Group acquired the former B&O Dover line between Clinton and Uhrichsville from CSX Transportation in December 1988. Corman trains interchange freight with CSX Transportation at Clinton. Three Corman locomotives are shown working in the CSX Transportation yard at Clinton on May 25, 1996. (Photograph by Richard Antibus.)

Ohio Central Railroad owns no track in Summit County, but uses trackage rights on R. J. Corman Railroad Group between Clinton and North Beach City. Much of the traffic interchanged with CSX Transportation is steel cars that originate at a steel mill at Butler, Pennsylvania, and are bound for a plant in Zanesville. The steel train is shown at Clinton with Warwick Tower visible to the right. (Photograph by Roger Durfee.)

Factories that received large numbers of railroad cars or had an extensive track network on their property often owned a switch engine. Akron tire makers Firestone and Goodyear once operated steam switchers, but Goodyear gave theirs up because of high labor costs. The tire makers relied on railroads serving their plants to do the switching. The nuclear energy division of Babcock and Wilcox in Barberton owned two diesel switchers. No. 1, a General Electric–built 44-tonner featured a center cab design typical of industrial switchers (seen in the photograph above). Shown in the photograph below is No. 8188, a rare Whitcomb-designed, Eddystone-built, 50-ton S3. Babcock and Wilcox did a lot of work for the federal government and it was common to see Department of Defense freight cars at the plant. (Above, photograph by Richard Antibus; below, photograph by Roger Durfee.)

The Pittsburgh Plate Glass Chemical Division in Barberton also owned a 70-ton switch engine, built by General Electric in February 1951. No. 9 was painted in a patriotic bicentennial livery in early 1976 and continued to wear those colors for several years. The Pittsburgh Plate Glass Chemical Division closed most of its Barberton operations in 1984. (Photograph by Richard Antibus.)

A brutal 1977 winter severely disrupted railroad operations in Ohio. Amtrak's Chicago–New York Broadway Limited, which ordinarily operated via Canton, detoured in February through Akron. The train is shown on the former Pennsylvania Railroad behind a trio of SDP40F locomotives. That same month, Amtrak's New York–Kansas City National Limited, which normally operated via Columbus and Dayton, detoured through Akron. (Photograph by Roger Durfee.)

When Amtrak began on May 1, 1971, the closest station to Akron was in Canton. A downgrading of the Conrail route used by the Broadway Limited in Ohio and Indiana forced it to move to the former B&O route between Chicago and Pittsburgh via Akron. A publicity train arrives at Akron's Quaker Square on November 7, 1990. Scheduled service began November 12. (Photograph by Edward Ribinskas.)

The September 10, 1995, discontinuance of the Broadway Limited left Akron without rail passenger service. Growing mail and express business prompted Amtrak to extend its New York–Pittsburgh Three Rivers to Chicago on November 10, 1996. The train did not begin serving Akron until August 10, 1998, due to the lack of a station. The eastbound Three Rivers departs Akron six hours late on January 23, 2005. (Photograph by Peter Bowler.)

The Cuyahoga Valley Preservation and Scenic Railway Association was formed in 1972 to provide excursion train service to the Cuyahoga Valley National Park on the former B&O Valley line. The Midwest Railway Historical Foundation of Cleveland provided passenger cars and steam locomotive 4070. Service began in 1975. American Locomotive Company built the 2-8-2 light Mikado in December 1918 for the Grand Trunk Western, and it hauled freight until March 29, 1960. The Midwest Railway Historical Foundation acquired the 4070 in 1966. Except when service was suspended in 1986 and 1987, the 4070 pulled excursion trains through 1990. The 4070 passes beneath the Ohio Route 82 bridge over the Cuyahoga River, near Brecksville on October 31, 1988 (seen in the photograph above), and is near Howard Street in Akron (seen in the photograph below) in 1984. (Above, photograph by Marty Surdyk; below, photograph by John Schon.)

The Cuyahoga Valley Scenic Railroad began acquiring diesel locomotives in 1988 and has operated with a variety of locomotives and passenger equipment. For several years, locomotives wore a livery inspired by the Delaware and Hudson Railroad. FPA-4 No. 15, shown at Pleasant Valley Road in August 1993, is wearing the Delaware and Hudson Railroad–inspired scheme. The Cuyahoga Valley Scenic Railroad acquired No. 15 and sister locomotive No. 14 in 1993–1994. (Photograph by Marty Surdyk.)

The engineer has the whistle cord in hand as FPA-4 No. 14 approaches a crossing on the Cuyahoga Valley Scenic Railroad. Built in 1959 by the Montreal Locomotive Works for Canadian National, No. 14 was one of just 36 FPA locomotives built. Usually assigned to Montreal–Toronto high-speed service, No. 14 later pulled trains for VIA Rail Canada. (Photograph by Craig Sanders.)

The Cuyahoga Valley Scenic Railroad initially operated with coaches leased from the Midwest Railway Historical Foundation, but later acquired four former Canadian National Railroad cars. Observation car St. Lucie Sound was built for the Florida East Coast Railway and acquired by the Cuyahoga Valley Scenic Railroad in 1995. The car features a bar, sleeper rooms, and a lounge area. Etched glass panels add a touch of elegance. (Photograph by Craig Sanders.)

Cuyahoga Valley Scenic Railroad trains carry hikers, bicyclists, sightseers, and picnickers to Cuyahoga Valley National Park, but some passengers are bound for Akron and Canton cultural and educational institutions. A recent addition has been wine-tasting trains. Passengers board a Canton-bound train in Akron on June 19, 2004, led by No. 365, an Alco C420 built in 1965 for the Atlantic Coast line. (Photograph by Craig Sanders.)

Since the early 1970s, the Akron area has hosted numerous excursion trains, many offering vintage steam locomotives. In 1967, one hundred Akron residents raised $40,000 to purchase 4-8-4 Northern Type No. 2102 from the Reading Company. The T-1 locomotive was refurbished at a former Pennsylvania Railroad roundhouse behind the Firestone Plant, but plans to offer excursions snagged because no railroad agreed to host the trips. The AC&Y finally agreed to allow a 16-car train to run between Akron and Spencer, and the first excursions occurred April 24 and 25, 1971 (seen in the photograph above). The trips attracted nearly 2,000 passengers. The 2102, built in 1945, is shown in the photograph below in downtown Akron during a 1968 shakedown trip, pulling a tank car and Pennsylvania Railroad caboose. (Above, photograph by H. Vaughn Smith; below, photograph by Bob Farkas.)

To celebrate the 150th anniversary of the chartering of the B&O, the Chessie System, in 1977 and 1978, ran a series of excursions called the Chessie Steam Special. Leased passenger cars and steam locomotive 2101, a former Reading 4-8-4 Northern Type T-1 owned by Ross Rowland, were painted in the Chessie System's yellow and orange livery. The special is shown at Akron Junction. (Photograph by Bob Redmond.)

In 1993, Nickel Plate Road 2-8-4 No. 765 was given Chesapeake and Ohio Railway (C&O) markings and renumbered 2765 for a series of excursions on CSX Transportation. Like the original C&O 2765, No. 765 had been built by Lima Locomotive Works. Akron–Pittsburgh trips operated on the former Baltimore and Ohio (Akron–New Castle, Pennsylvania) and Pittsburgh and Lake Erie (New Castle–Pittsburgh). No. 2765 is in Akron on August 21, 1993. (Photograph by Edward Ribinskas.)

Some steam-powered excursions merely came through Akron. Such was the case on June 16, 1996, when Milwaukee Road Alco 4-8-4 class S3 No. 261 passed through en route to its Minnesota home, after having gone east in 1995 to help celebrate the grand opening of Steamtown in Scranton, Pennsylvania. The view is from the Thornton Street overpass. (Photograph by Marty Surdyk.)

Steam-powered excursions in the Akron area have become scarce in recent years, but diesel-powered trips have continued on the modern W&LE. A Mother's Day outing between Bellevue and Akron is shown at Akron on May 8, 1994. The two locomotives are adorned in a bright red and yellow livery, designed by W&LE employees and dubbed "the painted ladies." (Photograph by Craig Sanders.)

Nine

STREETCAR AND INTERURBAN RAILWAYS

Akron street railway service began August 18, 1883, when the Akron Street Railway and Herdic Company began horsecar service on South Main and Howard Streets. The Akron Street Railway put the city's first electric trolley into service on October 2, 1888. The Akron City Council in 1893 granted a franchise to the Akron and Cuyahoga Falls Rapid Transit Company, and by 1894, there were competing trolley services between Akron and Cuyahoga Falls.

The Akron, Bedford and Cleveland Railroad opened between Cleveland and Akron on November 10, 1895, the nation's first high-speed long-distance interurban between major cities. The newly formed Northern Ohio Traction Company acquired the Akron, Bedford and Cleveland Railroad on July 1, 1899, and the Akron Street Railway on February 18, 1901. The Northern Ohio Traction Company then bought Falls Rapid Transit, which by now operated between Barberton and Kent, on January 12, 1901.

The Northern Ohio Traction Company eventually reached south to Canton, Massillon, New Philadelphia, and Uhrichsville; west to Wadsworth; and east to Alliance and Warren. A new Akron terminal opened June 11, 1918, with an eight-track train shed and four-story headhouse. Per hour, 32 interurban trains on four routes entered or left the station.

The Northern Ohio Traction and Light Company (renamed in November 1902) peaked in the early 1920s, but increased competition from automobiles, trucks, and buses caused the freight and passenger business to sag. Akron–Canton service ended April 15, 1928. Ridership that year was 3.1 million, but had fallen to 1.5 million by 1931, when the Northern Ohio Power and Light Company (renamed on April 7, 1926) lost $156,713. The Ohio Public Utilities Commission gave the Northern Ohio Power and Light Company permission to end all remaining interurban service effective April 1, 1932.

On December 1, 1925, the Grant Street line was the first streetcar route converted to buses. All Akron city rail and bus lines were transferred in June 1930 to the Akron Transportation Company. More rail lines were abandoned or replaced by buses in the 1930s. The Office of Defense Transportation refused to allow Akron Transportation Company to convert its last rail line—Akron–Barberton—to trolleybuses during World War II. Service between Kenmore and Barberton ended May 19, 1946. Akron street railway cars operated for the final time on March 23, 1947.

The Akron Terminal train shed (seen in the photograph above) was linked to the waiting room by a tunnel. Trains arrived from Main Street through an alley and then entered one of the eight tracks as they turned northward. Departing trains headed toward Federal Street, before turning westward to go back to Main Street. Track 1 was used for baggage and express; Track 2 by Canton locals; Track 3 by Canton limiteds; Track 4 by Cleveland locals; Track 5 by Cleveland limiteds; Track 6 by Ravenna, Warren, and Alliance cars; Track 7 by Barberton and Wadsworth cars; and Track 8 by specials. Beginning in 1922, Tracks 1 and 2 were shared with buses. Pavement was laid between the rails. In this 1925 view, a Pennsylvania-Ohio bus for Youngstown waits next to two Cleveland cars. (Above, courtesy of Alex Bruchac collection; below, courtesy of James Spangler collection.)

The Akron and Cuyahoga Falls Rapid Transit Company completed a Kent extension on November 20, 1895. After Northern Ohio Traction Company acquired the Akron and Cuyahoga Falls Rapid Transit Company on February 18, 1901, the line was extended to Ravenna. The first car from Akron to Ravenna is shown on November 15, 1901, on North Water Street in Kent. Service on this route ended on March 31, 1932. (Courtesy of James Spangler collection.)

The New Philadelphia extension opened in August 1902. Cleveland–New Philadelphia limiteds began in March 1911, making the 94-mile trip in 4 hours and 10 minutes. Low population south of Canton made the route the weakest in the Northern Ohio system. Car 1501 was built by G. C. Kuhlman Car Company of Cleveland in 1920. The crew poses at the Ninth Street siding in Cleveland. (Courtesy of James Spangler collection.)

Akron-Cleveland interurban service was hourly when it began November 11, 1885, but expanded to every 20 minutes in December 1886. The running time was 2 hours and 40 minutes, but was reduced in 1896. In November 1927, Cleveland–Akron service was cut to 75 minutes, the fastest time between those cities. Car No. 48, built by G. C. Kuhlman Car Company in 1913, is shown in downtown Akron. (Courtesy of Alex Bruchac collection.)

The Canton-Akron Railway Company was the dream of William H. Hoover, owner of a North Canton saddle leather company and later of vacuum cleaner fame. Akron–Canton service began May 16, 1902, and ended April 15, 1928. This first major Northern Ohio Power and Light Company abandonment of passenger service isolated the northern lines from the southern end. St. Louis Car Company built No. 5 as a combine in 1902. (Courtesy of Alex Bruchac collection.)

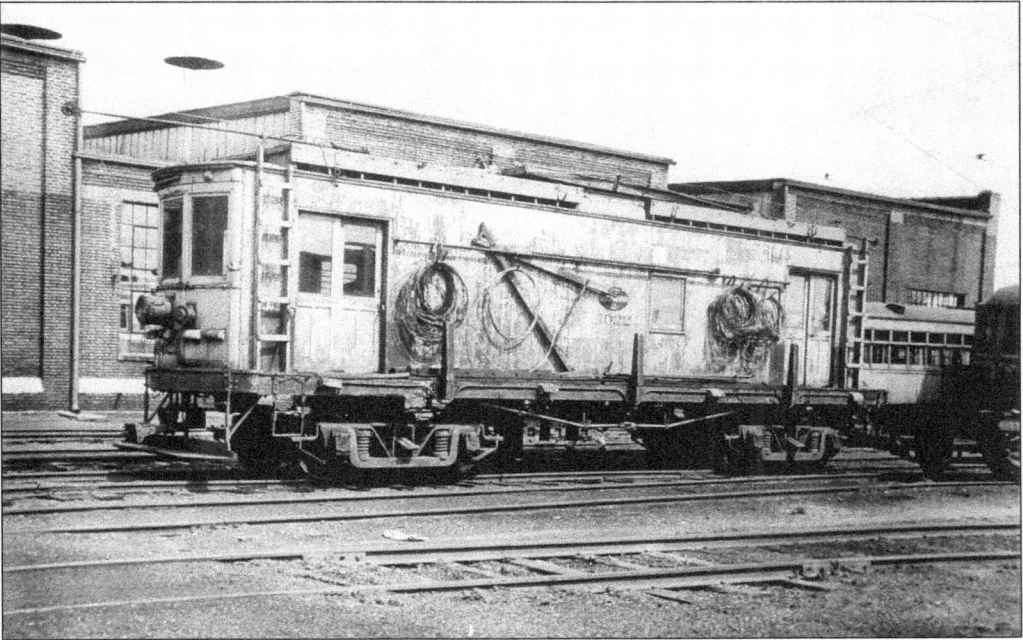

Interurban railways not only had to maintain tracks and stations just like steam railroads, but also had to keep hundreds of miles of overhead wires in good repair. Many interurban railways used a wire car to repair and perform maintenance on their systems. Northern Ohio Traction and Light Company used the wire car shown here. (Courtesy of Alex Bruchac collection.)

Most interurban railways handled freight and some interchanged cars with steam railroads. The Northern Ohio Power and Light Company freight fleet had reached a record 22 box motors and 60 freight trailers by 1929. The Northern Ohio Power and Light Company's freight business held up well through the late 1920s, when diversion to trucks and the Great Depression took their toll. The Northern Ohio Power and Light Company ceased handling freight on June 30, 1931. (Courtesy of Alex Bruchac collection.)

In 1926, the Northern Ohio Power and Light Company rebuilt 30 G. C. Kuhlman Car Company all-steel cars, making them more like steam railroad coaches. The cars received large picture windows, and comfortable seats replaced the original bench-style seating. These cars were assigned to limited trains between Cleveland and New Philadelphia, with some cars assigned to Akron–Ravenna service. These cars were well maintained until the 1932 end of service. (Courtesy of James Spangler collection.)

After ending passenger service on March 31, 1932, Northern Ohio Power and Light Company sold all 30 of its G. C. Kuhlman Car Company–built 1500 series luxury coaches. While the cars were used for a variety of purposes, some of them wound up being converted into diners. The Blue Ribbon Diner was located in Canal Fulton along U.S. Route 21. (Courtesy of James Spangler collection.)

Competing streetcar companies operated between Akron and Cuyahoga Falls, but not without a fight. Akron and Cuyahoga Falls Rapid Transit tried in 1894 to blow up the Akron Street Railroad bridge over Big Cuyahoga gorge. When that failed, Akron and Cuyahoga Falls Rapid Transit had the sheriff blockade the bridge. Akron Street Railroad (Falls Railroad), however, had unloaded a car on the other side and began service on existing track. Akron Street Railroad failed to persuade the Akron City Council to bar Akron and Cuyahoga Falls Rapid Transit operations in Akron. The two lines also vied to serve amusement parks and picnic groves. Ridership success sometimes hinged on the park being open on Sunday and/or allowing beer sales. An open-air Akron and Cuyahoga Falls Rapid Transit car is shown at what is believed to be Randolph Park (seen in the photograph above) while an Akron–Cuyahoga Falls car poses in an undated photograph. (Courtesy of Alex Bruchac collection.)

No. 12, the Barberton loop, left downtown Akron on South Main Street, switched to Kenmore Boulevard, and entered Barberton on North Wooster Road. Route 13 cars used the same route, continuing to Wadsworth until service ended December 31, 1934. A two-car train is shown passing the Kenmore shops on October 8, 1920. (Courtesy of James Spangler collection.)

Northern Ohio Traction Company gained a monopoly on Akron streetcar service on January 12, 1901, but spun off the city lines in June 1930 to Akron Transportation Company. City and interurban cars shared the same tracks in Akron. Wooster line and Barberton loop cars are shown in May 1929 on South Main Street, looking northward from Mill Street. Service ended on the Wooster line on June 11, 1932. (Courtesy of James Spangler collection.)

Interurban and streetcar lines sought to avoid grade crossings with steam railroads, but that was not always possible. Akron Transportation Company car 2041 operating on the East Market Street line, is shown crossing the AC&Y with a soap box derby special. Four routes once used East Market Street, but the last service east of Ellet was discontinued on May 9, 1934. (Courtesy of James Spangler collection.)

Streetcar service to Barberton ended May 19, 1946. Barberton Chamber of Commerce members dressed up as a barbershop quartet and about 100 automobiles chased the last trip, which ended in Barberton at 1:15 a.m. with 10 aboard. Some wore 1890s-style clothing and sang "Auld Lang Syne." A Barberton-bound car is shown in Kenmore on October 17, 1945. Note the movie poster by the front door. (Courtesy of James Spangler collection.)

Akron gained its first Peter Witt cars on June 10, 1925. Designed and named for a Cleveland transit executive, the cars featured center doors and one-man operation. Akron Transportation Company rebuilt several cars during World War II, installing new trucks and floors. Cars 2028 and 2017 are on Market Street between Main and High Streets. The man running at left is Akron Railroad Club cofounder Robert Richardson. (Photograph by John Wunderle.)

The last stand for Akron streetcars was the route to stop 97 in Kenmore. Ridership had risen during the World War II years, but Akron Transportation Company wanted to replace its last 12 streetcars with trolley buses. Street railway service in Akron ended on March 23, 1947, after 65 years. A lone car makes its way along Kenmore Boulevard in happier times. (Courtesy of James Spangler collection.)

Ten

AKRON RAILROAD CLUB

During the 1930s, *Railroad* magazine published rail fan trip reports. Reading these accounts gave some Akron men an idea. Robert Richardson, Bruce Triplett, Kenneth Richards, and Robert McFarland formed a committee in 1936 to explore arranging fan trips in Ohio. The National Railway Historical Society had been born in Philadelphia a year earlier, and in June 1937, the Akron committee became the Eastern Ohio Chapter of the National Railway Historical Society. Richardson was elected president.

Some efforts to arrange trips ended in frustration. The AC&Y refused to run a special train, and the Pennsylvania Railroad demanded a minimum of 125 regular fares, which the fledgling club could ill afford. The Lisbon and Western Railroad agreed to charter its gasoline-electric car for $30, but refused to allow photography.

Interurban railways proved more receptive because many were struggling financially and welcomed the charter trip revenue. Among the early trips were an outing on the Stark Electric Railroad between Canton and Salem and two trips on the Lake Shore Electric Railway before it halted operations in 1938. Some trips turned a profit, but others lost money.

Monthly meetings were held in members' homes. There was plenty of railroad talk and usually railroad movies. Attendance seldom topped 25. Typically the host would hang a railroad lantern outside for identification and serve sandwiches and refreshments. In June 1940, the chapter launched a monthly newsletter, the *Bulletin*.

A November 1945 referendum favored dropping the National Railway Historical Society affiliation and the club renamed itself Northeastern Ohio Railfans. Several members soon had second thoughts about that name, and at the March 27, 1947, meeting, the group reorganized as the Akron Railroad Club.

Much has changed since the club's early years. Movies have given way to slide shows and digital photographs. Lack of interest by the railroads and rising costs have restricted the opportunities for fan trips. Today most Akron Railroad Club trips involve photographing and watching trains at various railroad hot spots in Ohio, Pennsylvania, or Michigan. Membership has grown to more than 100, making the Akron Railroad Club one of the largest railroad enthusiast groups in northeast Ohio.

Akron Railroad Club member Bill Schriber owned a 15-inch gauge miniature railroad at his home in Massillon that he called the back and front yard railroad. Members of the Eastern Ohio Chapter of the National Railway Historical Society were frequent guests on the back and front yard railroad during World War II, when railroads ceased offering fan trips. In the photograph above, Schriber is shown at the throttle of one of his steam locomotives. In the photograph below, engineer John Holt takes Eastern Ohio Chapter members for a ride. At far left are John and Marjorie Clark. After John entered the Army in late 1943, Marjorie became the acting *Bulletin* editor in her husband's absence. The back and front yard railroad later moved to a site near Navarre. (Photographs by Glenn G. Grabill; courtesy of John B. Corns collection.)

Regular streetcar service operated between downtown Akron and Ellet for the last time on November 12, 1941, but four days later the Eastern Ohio Chapter of the National Railway Historical Society operated a farewell excursion to Ellet. Chapter member John Wunderle poses in front of the chartered car. Wunderle and Robert Richardson are the only surviving Eastern Ohio Chapter members in the Akron Railroad Club. (Courtesy of John Wunderle collection.)

Kenneth Richards was one of the members of the committee formed in 1936 that evolved into the Akron Railroad Club. The men had a mutual interest in railroads and were surprised to find that they were not alone in having spent time watching railroad operations in Akron. Richards is shown on August 19, 1941, during an excursion on the Jamestown, Westfield and Northwestern Railroad. (Photograph by John Wunderle.)

Many of the early excursions sponsored by the Eastern Ohio Chapter involved interurban railway companies, which were often more willing to charter trains for railroad enthusiasts than were the steam railroads. The Jamestown, Westfield and Northwestern Railroad was one of the few interurbans that had an open platform car. Excursionists enjoy the view during an August 19, 1941, outing. (Courtesy of John Wunderle collection.)

Several interurban railways ceased operations in the 1940s, prompting Akron Railroad Club members to make farewell excursions before the cars went silent. The Youngstown and Southern was Ohio's last interurban railway and carried passengers for the final time on December 31, 1947. Club members are shown at Boardman during an excursion on August 3, 1947. The white flags indicate that this is an extra train. (Photograph by John Wunderle.)

THE LAKESIDE & MARBLEHEAD R. R., was opened for service in January, 1887, a few months after formation of the parent Kelly Island Lime & Transport Co. The line extends seven miles to a junction with the N. Y. C. at Danbury, with four miles of branches. Passenger service was discontinued in March, 1930. At that time Motor Car #5 said be the first McKeen gas car in Ohio, was in use. Thanks to Mr. O. F. Gardner, Manager, the car will be outside the storage shed for snapshots. A relic of steam passenger runs is the old #3 coach in rear of enginehouse, which last you may notice is for both gauges. Note where our car stops the unusual track designed for use of the three roads and both gauges. Mr. Gardner has also arranged the line-up of engines.

L. & M. R. R. ROSTER

Locomotives

0-6-0 5, 6, built by Dunkirk Wks., American Locomotive Co. 1912
0-6-0 7, 8, superheaters by Lima Locomotive Works, 1928

Freight and Work Cars

Box 501, 502   Flat 400-404   Dump 601-605

THE Eastern Ohio Chapter of The National Railway Historical Society was formed in the past year for the purpose of sponsoring field trips like this, to encourage collecting of railway historical material, and to foster support by the general public of our railroads. Membership is open to anyone interested in railways. Annual dues

EASTERN OHIO CHAPTER

National Railway
HISTORICAL SOCIETY

Railway "Fan" Excursion

in

Old Number 21

The Eastern Ohio Chapter's first steam excursion occurred October 17, 1937. A chartered Ohio Public Service Company interurban car took participants from Toledo to Marblehead, where Kelleys Island and Transport Company had a fleet of steam locomotives for a quarry operation. Some rode in the locomotive cab during the three-mile trip. Others rode in a boxcar with bench seats. Shown here is the trip guide cover. (Courtesy of John Wunderle collection.)

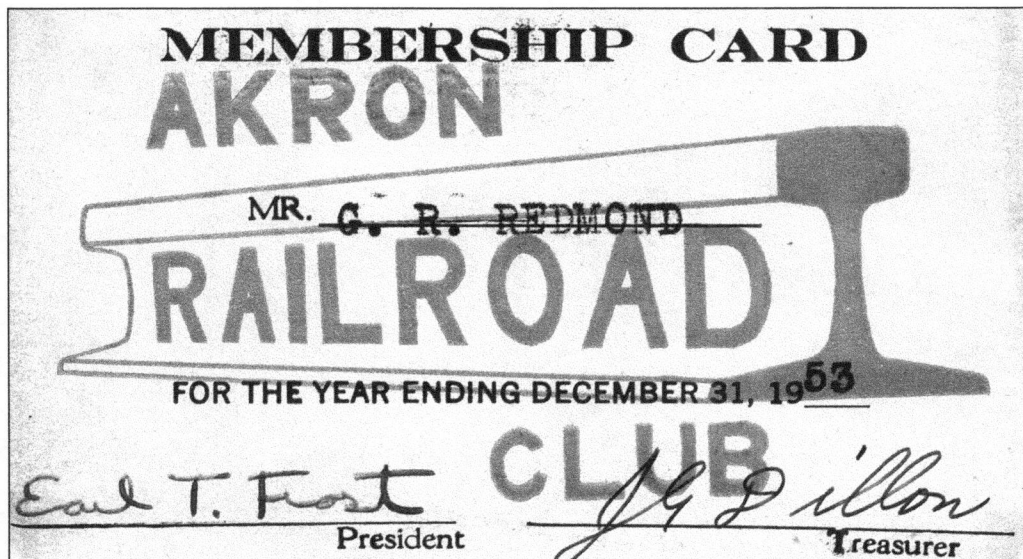

A few months after reorganizing as the Akron Railroad Club in 1947, members approved a club logo featuring the club name and a length of rail. The logo was used for the *Bulletin*, stationery, tickets, and membership cards. This logo was used through the early 1950s. (Courtesy of Bob Redmond collection.)

Akron Railroad Club members had a New Year's Day tradition of riding the AC&Y mixed train between Akron and New London. Club members are shown January 2, 1950, at Spencer, waiting for the train to finish switching. The trip occurred on January 2 because the train did not operate on Sunday, which fell on New Year's Day in 1950. (Photograph by Bob Redmond.)

Akron Railroad Club members ranged far and wide to ride trains in the club's early years. Members did not have to go far in January 1957 for an outing on the Shaker Heights Rapid in Cleveland. Akron Railroad Club members are waiting for the transit car to make a photograph runby. (Photograph by Bob Redmond.)

THE AKRON RAILROAD CLUB

☆ PRESENTS ☆

GREENVILLE TO N. BESSEMER & RETURN

"RAILFAN TRIP"

SUNDAY JUNE 26, 1955
LV. GREENVILLE, PA.
8:30 A. M. D. S. T.

Via

BESSEMER

& LAKE ERIE R.R.

INCLUDES PHOTO STOPS
AND GUIDED INSPECTION
TOUR of GREENVILLE SHOP

| 0055 | GOING | RETURN | HALF FARE |

The Akron Railroad Club conducted its first outing to visit the Bessemer and Lake Erie Railroad in 1947. Although the railroad agreed to allow the club to visit its Greenville, Pennsylvania, shops and roundhouse, it prohibited photography. The Bessemer and Lake Erie was owned by a steel company at the time, and many steel plants would not allow photographing of their factories or railroads. However, club members circumvented the ban during a trip on a Bessemer and Lake Erie passenger train to Erie, Pennsylvania. The conductor stopped the train next to an open field, and members disembarked and shot photographs with management none the wiser. By the time of the Bessemer and Lake Erie excursion on June 26, 1955, however, management had changed its mind about photography. In the photograph below, members are shown photographing their diesel-powered excursion train. (Courtesy of Bob Redmond collection.)

A tradition of Akron Railroad Club outings is taking a group photograph. During an outing to visit a trolley museum in Johnstown, Pennsylvania, in 1958, Akron Railroad Club members pose next to a transit car. Shown are, from left to right, Bob Curtis, Fred Roe, Hazel Roe, Bob Redmond, unidentified, William Kuethe Sr., J. Gary Dillon, John Alden, Bruce Triplett, an unidentified motorman, Triplett's daughter Jean, and John Stein. (Courtesy of Marty Surdyk collection.)

In the 1960s, the Akron Railroad Club chartered a B&O rail diesel car for an outing from Akron to Sandusky, home of the Cedar Point amusement park. The two-car train stopped at the gate to the ferry to the park. Helen Kuethe and her niece Cheryl Megenhardt enjoy the ride. Cedar Point remains today, but the B&O line to Sandusky is gone. (Photograph by William Kuethe Sr.)

The decline of intercity passenger service led to diminished opportunities for Akron Railroad Club members to ride scheduled trains. When possible, Akron Railroad Club members continue to plan outings on Amtrak, although the closest station is in Cleveland. Shown on an October 1978 trip to South Bend aboard Amtrak's Lake Shore Limited are, from left to right, Charlie Averill, Clint Ensworth, Tom Redmond, and Bob Redmond. (Photograph by H. Vaughn Smith.)

On December 18, 1947, eighteen Akron Railroad Club members and their wives attended the first Christmas banquet held at the Seven Gables restaurant in Fairlawn. Banquet speakers have included railroad executives, photographers, authors, and magazine editors. George Badstuber (left) and Jerry Jacobson, longtime Akron Railroad Club member and chairman of the Ohio Central Railroad, are engrossed in a conversation during a 1970s-era banquet. (Photograph by H. Vaughn Smith.)

The Akron Railroad Club combined forces with the Forest City Division of the Railroad Enthusiasts on April 26, 1987, to sponsor an excursion on the New York and Lake Erie Railroad. Members of the two clubs enjoyed riding in a specially outfitted gondola that was ideal for sightseeing and photography. The train is about to stop at Cherry Creek, New York, for a photograph runby. (Photograph by Edward Ribinskas.)

During the 1990s and early 21st century, the Ohio Central Railroad hosted an annual steam-powered excursion for the Akron Railroad Club. Ohio Central Railroad steam locomotives 13 and 1293 smoke it up for the photograph line during a runby at Barrs Mills on October 11, 1997. The excursions usually ran in October. (Photograph by Edward Ribinskas.)

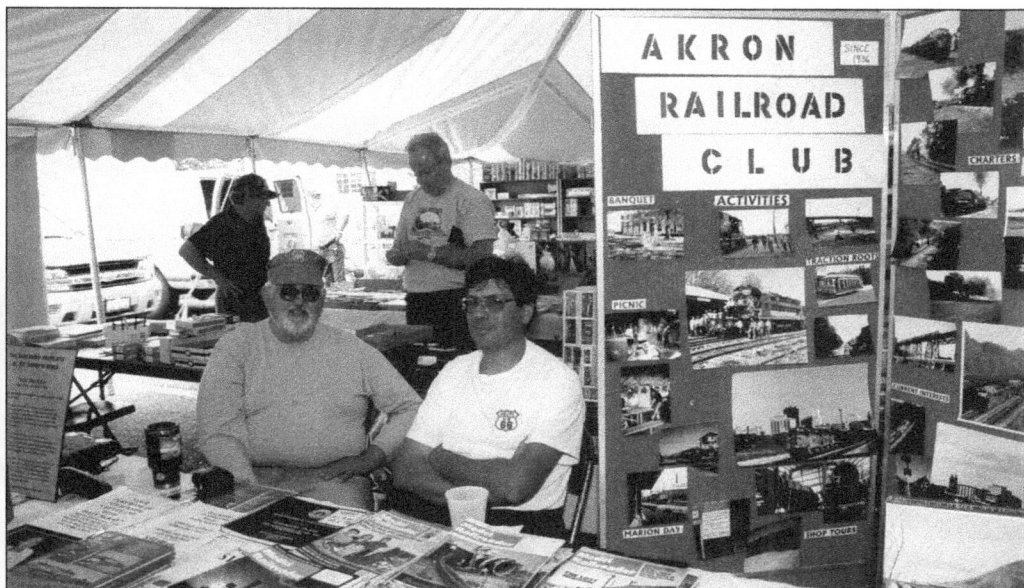

Railroad shows are an ideal place to recruit new members, so the Akron Railroad Club sets up a display at various shows in northeast Ohio. Aside from providing information about club activities, the club also sells magazines, books, and photographs. Rick Houck (left) and Marty Surdyk staff the Akron Railroad Club table during depot days in Orrville, in June 2006. (Photograph by Richard Jacobs.)

The summer picnic is an Akron Railroad Club tradition. The July 2005 outing was held at the Northern Ohio Railway Museum. Shown are, from left to right, Dennis Tharp, Michael Dick, Karen Dick (kneeling), Tasha the dog, William Dick (kneeling), Craig Sanders, Clint Ensworth, Mark Adamcik, Robert MacCallum, Eli Rantanes and his grandchildren Cecily and Chelsie Lent (standing in front), Marty Surdyk, Todd Vander Sluis, and J. Gary Dillon. (Photograph by Richard Jacobs.)

Visit us at
arcadiapublishing.com

www.ingramcontent.com/pod-product-compliance
Lightning Source LLC
Chambersburg PA
CBHW080547110426
42813CB00006B/1232